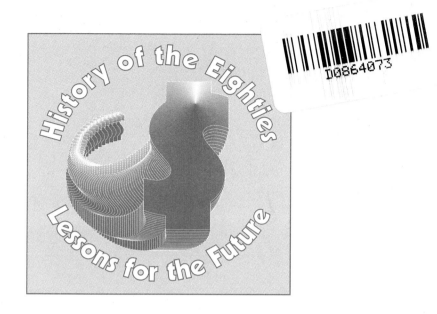

Volume II

Symposium Proceedings

January 16, 1997

Federal Deposit Insurance Corporation

First published by the Federal Deposit Insurance Corporation in 1997.

This publication may be obtained electronically via the Internet at:
http://www.fdic.gov/databank/hist80

ISBN 0-9661808-0-1 (2 Volume Set)

Library of Congress Catalog Card Number: 97-77644.

Contents

History of the Eighties—Lessons for the Future
Federal Deposit Insurance Corporation
January 16, 1997
Agenda

8:45 to 9:15 A.M.	**Introduction and Overview** *William R. Watson, Director, Division of Research and Statistics, FDIC*
9:15 to 10:30 A.M.	**Examination and Enforcement** A review and analysis of the effectiveness of federal bank examination, supervision, and enforcement actions during the 1980s and early 1990s. *Introduction: William R. Watson, Director, DRS, FDIC* *Moderator: Nicholas J. Ketcha Jr., Director, Division of Supervision, FDIC* *Presenter: James F. Freund, Chief, DRS Economic Analysis Section, FDIC*

8:45 to 9:15 A.M.

Introduction and Overview

William R. Watson, Director, Division of Research and Statistics, FDIC

9:15 to 10:30 A.M.

Examination and Enforcement

A review and analysis of the effectiveness of federal bank examination, supervision, and enforcement actions during the 1980s and early 1990s.

Introduction: William R. Watson, Director, DRS, FDIC
Moderator: Nicholas J. Ketcha Jr., Director, Division of Supervision, FDIC
Presenter: James F. Freund, Chief, DRS Economic Analysis Section, FDIC

Discussants: *R. Alton Gilbert, Federal Reserve Bank of St. Louis*
Gary Gorton, The Wharton School
Joe Peek, Boston College
Stephen R. Steinbrink, Former Deputy Comptroller, OCC

10:45 to 12:00 P.M.

Off-Site Surveillance Systems

Effectiveness of financial reporting and off-site risk monitoring in anticipating bank problems and directing supervisory resources during the 1980s and early 1990s.

Introduction: William R. Watson, Director, DRS, FDIC
Moderator: Arthur Murton, Director, Division of Insurance, FDIC
Presenter: Jack Reidhill, Chief, DRS Policy Research Section, FDIC

Discussants: *Robert Avery, Board of Governors*
Mark Flannery, University of Florida
Christopher M. James, University of Florida

12:00 to 1:30 P.M.   **Luncheon Presentation**
Keynote Speaker: Ricki Helfer, Chairman, FDIC*

1:30 to 2:45 P.M.   **Lessons of the 1980s: What Does the Evidence Show?**
Role of deposit insurance, market discipline, forbearance, early
intervention. Common threads in regional and sectoral crises and
regulatory responses. What can be done to reduce the severity of
future problems?
Introduction: William R. Watson, Director, DRS, FDIC
Moderator: L. William Seidman, Chief Commentator, CNBC
Presenter: George Hanc, Associate Director, DRS, FDIC
Discussants: Jonathan Fiechter, World Bank
Robert E. Litan, Brookings Institution
Stanley Silverberg, Banking Consultant
Lawrence J. White, New York University

3:00 to 4:15 P.M.   **The 1980s in Retrospect**
Introduction: Ricki Helfer, Chairman, FDIC
Moderator: Paul A. Volcker, BT Wolfensohn
Discussants: Carter Golembe, CHG Consulting
William Isaac, Secura Group
John G. Medlin, Jr., Wachovia Corporation

* Ricki Helfer left her position as Chairman of the FDIC in May 1997

Introduction

The FDIC sought comments from academics and other bank regulators on preliminary results of the FDIC's study at a symposium held on January 16, 1997, at which three draft papers were presented. These papers have since been revised, and now correspond to Chapters 1, 12, and 13 in Volume 1 of this study. Participants at the symposium were invited to provide written versions of their comments for publication, and those submitted are presented in this volume. In addition, the symposium's final panel included a less structured discussion, an edited transcript of which is presented. Finally, the keynote address of Ricki Helfer, then-Chairman of the FDIC, to the symposium is also included in this volume. These materials are organized according to the order of the symposium's agenda.

Readers should note that in the study the FDIC's Division of Research and Statistics sought to take into account the symposium participants' observations; the study therefore now often reflects those comments. In addition, readers should be aware that further analysis undertaken since the symposium has occasionally resulted in changes to the materials upon which symposium participants based their comments.

The views expressed by the symposium participants are their own, and are not necessarily those of the Federal Deposit Insurance Corporation.

Panel 1

Examination and Enforcement

R. Alton Gilbert
Joe Peek
Stephen R. Steinbrink

Examination and Enforcement

Comment on Examination and Enforcement
R. Alton Gilbert*

I commend the staff of the FDIC for preparing the papers in this volume on the problems of banking in the 1980s. These papers present information not available from other sources. The paper on examination and enforcement (FDIC, 1997a), in particular, presents information on the record of examinations of troubled banks and the enforcement actions of supervisors that is not available from other sources. I will give my opinion on whether the paper draws the correct lessons for the future from the history of the 1980s.

Conclusions about Banking in the 1980s

I agree with most of the conclusions in the paper:

- Among banks examined frequently, CAMEL ratings were accurate indicators of problems at most of the banks that failed.

- CAMEL ratings were less reliable indicators of the condition of banks examined less frequently.[1]

- The behavior of most of the banks that supervisors identified as troubled banks was consistent with that desired by the supervisors: these banks reduced their assets and dividend rates. In general, banks did not take the kinds of actions that supervisors associate with greater risk after the supervisors had identified their problems.[2]

---

* The author is Vice President at the Federal Reserve Bank of St. Louis. The views expressed are those of the author, and do not necessarily reflect those of the Federal Reserve Bank of St. Louis or the Federal Reserve System.

[1] These first two conclusions are consistent with those of my studies of bank examinations; see Gilbert (1993, 1994).

[2] For other evidence on this point, see Gilbert (1991).

- In most cases supervisors acted to restrict the behavior of troubled banks before they would have been required to act under the scheme for prompt corrective action in FDICIA, which became law in 1991.[3]

- If the requirement in FDICIA for early closure of critically undercapitalized banks had been imposed during the 1980s, the cost savings of the FDIC would have been small relative to total resolution costs during that period.

Estimating the Cost of Delayed Closure

I have some additional comments on the last point about the costs to the FDIC of letting critically undercapitalized banks remain in operation. First, the results of one of my studies do not support the argument that FDIC resolution costs were positively related to the length of time that banks operated with relatively low capital ratios prior to their failure (Gilbert [1992]). Second, I have reasons to believe that the estimate in the FDIC's paper overstates the costs to the FDIC of permitting critically undercapitalized banks to remain in operation beyond the period permitted in FDICIA.

The FDIC estimates this cost for each of the critically undercapitalized banks that eventually failed by summing its operating expenses and the excess of its funding costs over yields on Treasury securities for the period it remained in operation beyond that permitted under FDICIA. This extra period was not long for most of the 340 critically undercapitalized banks that eventually failed; the median period was two quarters.

It is likely that many of these 340 banks were closed under arrangements that involved bids from other banks for their assets or uninsured deposits, since most resolutions during this period involved such bids (see Bovenzi and Muldoon [1990]). Resolutions that involved bids from other banks generally were less costly to the FDIC (see Bovenzi and Murton [1988] and Gilbert [1992]) but take more time to arrange than closing failed banks and making payments to their insured depositors. During much of the 1980s, the staffs of the bank supervisory agencies had difficulty keeping pace with the rate of bank closings. Earlier closure of these 340 banks, therefore, probably would have required more failed-bank cases to be resolved by closing the banks and paying their insured deposit liabilities. Thus, in the environment of the 1980s, when the number of banks in terminal financial condition was taxing the ability of supervisors to arrange orderly resolu-

---

[3] See Peek and Rosengren (1996b, 1997) for more evidence.

tions, earlier closure of critically undercapitalized banks that eventually failed probably would not have saved the FDIC as much as the paper estimated.

Effects of Formal Enforcement Actions

Another conclusion of the FDIC paper is that formal enforcement actions had about the same effects on the behavior of problem banks as informal actions. Table 1 presents some of the FDIC's evidence, which contrasts the growth rates in total assets, dividend rates and capital injections for the problem banks subject to formal and informal enforcement actions.[4] Since these measures of behavior were about the same for the two groups of banks, the paper concludes that the step of imposing formal enforcement actions on problem banks had no effect on their behavior.

I do not find the evidence convincing. Some of my concerns involve measurement issues. One measurement issue involves the timing of the formal enforcement actions. The FDIC provides no information on the timing of the formal enforcement actions relative to these periods in Table 1 of three years, two years and one year prior to failure. To illustrate the problem, suppose no formal enforcement actions were imposed on the problem banks as early as three years prior to their failure. In that case, we would not expect significant effects of formal enforcement actions on the behavior of problem banks three years prior to their failure.

The choice of denominator for the dividends ratio probably amplifies noise in the observations, another type of measurement problem. Net income tends to be more variable over time for problem banks than for other banks, with large drops in the net income of problem banks, or possibly losses, in the quarters when they make large provisions for loan losses. High variance in the ratios of dividends to net income tends to reduce the statistical significance of differences between the means of dividends ratios for the two groups of banks. Total assets would be a better denominator for the dividends ratio.

Another concern about inferences drawn from Table 1 involves an assumption implicit in the design of the table that supervisors distributed formal enforcement actions randomly among problem banks. I have an alternative assumption about how supervisors determined which banks were subjected to formal en-

---

[4] Readers should note that in Chapter 12 in volume 1 of this study the manner in which these data are presented has been changed; some changes have also been made in the way the data are calculated (FDIC's note).

Table 1

The Effects of FDIC Enforcement Actions Upon the Asset Growth Rates, Dividend Payments and Capital Injections of FDIC Problem Banks 1980-1994

(Problem banks: those with CAMEL ratings of 4 or 5)

Years Prior to Failure	Failed banks subject to formal enforcement actions	
	Yes	No
Percentage change in total assets		
3 years	14.81 %	10.29 %
2 years	1.90	3.97*
1 year	−6.83	−7.85
Dividends as percentage of net income		
3 years	21.12 %	34.37 %
2 years	7.58	74.20
1 year	2.54	−3.53
Capital Injections as percentage of total assets		
3 years	0.33 %	0.48 %
2 years	0.45	0.39
1 year	0.39	0.38

* Difference in mean statistically significant at the 5 percent level.

forcement actions: those that exhibited relatively poor compliance with informal enforcement actions became subject to formal actions. Some observations in the FDIC's paper are consistent with my assumption. About half of the problem banks were subjected to formal actions. The median period between the date of the examination when a bank was rated CAMEL 4 or 5 and the effective date of a formal enforcement action was about two-thirds of a year. Thus, FDIC supervisors were selective in imposing formal enforcement actions, and they took a long time to decide which banks would be subjected to the formal actions.

Suppose supervisors judged the compliance of problem banks with informal enforcement actions in terms of their asset growth, dividends and capital injections. If so, we should measure the effects of formal enforcement actions by focusing on these measures for problem banks before and after they were subjected to formal enforcement actions. Peek and Rosengren (1995a 1995b, 1996a), who use this approach, find significant effects of formal enforcement actions on bank behavior.

Lessons for the Future

I draw the following lessons for the future from the history of the 1980s:

- Maintain the schedule of on-site examinations.

- While some improvement of examination procedures may be possible, it is not necessary to make radical changes in examinations to provide supervisors with reliable information on the condition of banks.

- Since supervisors act more promptly in dealing with troubled banks than required by the prompt corrective action provisions of FDICIA, this legislation has not eliminated the need for supervisors to exercise judgment in using their powers. Supervisors will continue to be criticized for the way they exercise their judgment: at times accused of forbearance, and at other times accused of being overly restrictive.

- Implementation of supervision as required in FDICIA will not eliminate losses to the FDIC fund in the future.

It is important that public officials outside of supervision become aware of these lessons for the future. It would be unfortunate if, during a future period of problems in the banking industry, supervisors are distracted from their work by having to explain to public officials why they are exercising judgment, and why bank failures are imposing losses on the deposit insurance fund.

The paper presented by Hanc (FDIC, 1997b) deals with the most important challenge for supervision at this time: limiting the risk assumed by banks when they are profitable and classified as "well capitalized." The experience of the 1980s indicates that over time large losses and failures reflect risks assumed by banks when their profits and capital ratios made them appear financially strong.

Supervisors are modifying examination procedures to focus on risk management. New examination procedures, however, do not provide supervisors with the will to use their powers to limit the risk assumed by banks while they are profitable and well capitalized. Unless supervisors are effective in developing these procedures and effective in using them to limit risk, they will have failed to respond to the most important lesson of the 1980s.

References

Bovenzi, John F. and Arthur J. Murton. "Resolution Costs of Bank Failures," *FDIC Banking Review* (Fall 1988), pp. 1-13.

Bovenzi, John F. and Maureen D. Muldoon. "Failure-Resolution Methods and Policy Considerations," *FDIC Banking Review* (Fall 1990), pp. 1-11.

Federal Deposit Insurance Corporation. "Bank Examination and Enforcement, 1980-1994." Draft of Chapter 12 (December 1996) in *History of the Eighties—Lessons for the Future*, Vol. 1 (1997a).

Federal Deposit Insurance Corporation. "A Summary of the Project Findings." Draft of Chapter 1 (December 1996) in *History of the Eighties—Lessons for the Future*, Vol. 1 (1997b).

Gilbert, R. Alton. "Supervision of Undercapitalized Banks: Is There a Case for Change?" Federal Reserve Bank of St. Louis *Review* (May/June 1991), pp. 16-30.

Gilbert, R. Alton. "The Effects of Legislating Prompt Corrective Action on the Bank Insurance Fund." Federal Reserve Bank of St. Louis *Review* (July/August 1991), pp. 3-22.

Gilbert, R. Alton. "Implications of Annual Examinations for the Bank Insurance Fund." Federal Reserve Bank of St. Louis *Review* (January/February 1993), pp. 35-52.

Gilbert, R. Alton. "The Benefits of Annual Bank Examinations." *Research in Financial Services*, JAI Press (1994), pp. 215-48.

Peek, Joe and Eric. S. Rosengren. "Banks and the Availability of Small Business Loans." Working Paper No. 95-1, Federal Reserve Bank of Boston (January 1995a).

Peek, Joe and Eric S. Rosengren. "Bank Regulation and the Credit Crunch." *Journal of Banking and Finance* (June 1995b), pp. 679-92.

Peek, Joe and Eric S. Rosengren. "The Use of Capital Ratios to Trigger Intervention in Problem Banks: Too Little, Too Late." *New England Economic Review* (September/October 1996b), pp. 49-58.

Peek, Joe and Eric S. Rosengren. "Bank Regulatory Agreements and Real Estate Lending." *Real Estate Economics*, Vol. 24 (1996a), pp. 55-73.

Peek, Joe and Eric S. Rosengren. "Will Legislated Early Intervention Prevent the Next Banking Crisis?" *Southern Economic Journal* (July 1997).

Comment on "Bank Examination and Enforcement, 1980-1994"
Joe Peek*

Even though a number of studies have looked at regulatory intervention and many more have investigated bank failures, we still do not understand nearly as much about the process as we could, and should. That is why I view the "History of the Eighties" project as an important contribution. The FDIC has undertaken the first (and most important) step: constructing a comprehensive database that merges heretofore incompatible data sets of examiner information, regulatory actions, and bank balance sheet and income statement information, and then turning their research staff loose on it to see what they could learn. Chairman Helfer took the well-worn phrase "It's a dirty job, but someone has to do it" and, unlike most other people, did not implicitly replace the word "someone" with "someone else." The result is a much-needed public service, and I applaud the FDIC for their efforts.

This project has also taken a necessary second step, promoting the interaction of two separate divisions within the regulatory agency, the examination and supervision division and the research division. These two groups, both at the FDIC and at the other bank regulatory agencies, traditionally have had only limited access to the expertise and information of the other. Certainly, they can learn much from each other.

How can we expect to write regulatory legislation and implement that legislation effectively if we do not understand exactly how banks react to intervention, or even the threat of intervention? And, more important, whether that reaction, in fact, reduces the probability of a bank failing, or, should the bank subsequently fail despite regulatory intervention, at least reduces the resolution cost to the FDIC. Increasing the flow of information between the examination and supervision divisions and the research divisions of the bank regulatory agencies has the potential to make substantial improvements in bank examination and enforcement, the topic of the paper under discussion.

---

* The author is Professor, Department of Economics, Boston College and Visiting Economist, Research Department, Federal Reserve Bank of Boston. The views expressed are those of the author, and do not necessarily reflect official positions of the Federal Reserve Bank of Boston or the Federal Reserve System.

Bank Examination and Enforcement, 1980 to 1994

This study has two main objectives: (1) to provide an historical account and evaluation of bank supervision policies and (2) to assess the effectiveness of bank supervisory tools in limiting losses to the bank insurance fund. The authors have done an admirable job on the first objective, and I presume the findings will be incorporated into their next budget request for additional examiner resources. I certainly agree that there is no substitute for on-site monitoring. In fact, "being there" can only become more important over time as ongoing trends in the banking industry—the movement to off-balance-sheet activities, the movement into nontraditional banking products, and the geographic expansion of operations, both domestically and globally—further complicate the lives of those in the supervision and regulation division.

With respect to the second component of the study, I find most of the results quite believable, in large part because they line up quite closely with the evidence that Eric Rosengren and I have found in a number of our studies. For example:

1. On-site exams are valuable for providing information to regulators and for maintaining the integrity of reported data. This result also confirms the findings in a series of papers by another member of the panel, Alton Gilbert.

2. On-site exams were reasonably effective in identifying troubled banks (Peek and Rosengren [1996]).

3. Prompt Corrective Action, as now implemented, is unlikely to impose much of a constraint on supervisory intervention; formal actions tend to be imposed well before most banks become undercapitalized according to PCA capital thresholds (Peek and Rosengren [1997]).

In addition, the study's suggestion that developments in the regional and national economy that could pose future problems be incorporated into failure models and into the exam process is on the right track.

On the other hand, I would be more reserved in my interpretation of the results with respect to the effectiveness of regulatory intervention. However, to paraphrase a line from the study's summary, these comments do not represent criticisms, but only serve to point out limitations to the analysis.

The analysis of the effectiveness of regulatory intervention should be broken into two separate questions. First, was regulatory intervention effective in changing bank behavior? And second, did that change in bank behavior reduce the probability of failure, or at least reduce the cost to the FDIC from those banks that did eventually fail? On the first issue, the authors find no consistent differences in asset growth rates between problem banks (rated CAMEL 4 or 5) that did receive formal actions and problem banks that did not. Yet, in considering the second issue, they suggest that regulatory intervention has been effective. They argue that essentially all problem banks are subject to intervention, so perhaps their result is really just telling us that informal intervention (in the form of a memorandum of understanding—MOU) is no less effective than a formal action.

In contrast, Eric Rosengren and I (Peek and Rosengren [1995]) have found fairly strong evidence that the imposition of formal regulatory actions—cease-and-desist orders and written agreements—did have an immediate and dramatic effect on loan and asset growth at banks in New England during the recent banking crisis. Since then, we have expanded our database to include banks nationwide and the results hold up, so that it was not simply a New England phenomenon. And these results are obtained while controlling for bank-specific characteristics, including measures of bank health.

The difference in our results may be related to a difference in the bank sample (all FDIC-regulated banks compared to our sample of all New England banks), but is more likely due to differences in methodology. The FDIC study uses the failure date or recovery date as the point of reference, while we use the date of the exam that resulted in the formal action as our reference point. I believe that the proper test is to treat the imposition of a formal action as an event, comparing bank behavior immediately before and after the event. Only in this way can one really determine whether the event had an effect on bank behavior. In any case, it is interesting that even though Eric and I appear to find the stronger evidence that regulatory intervention changed bank behavior, we remain much more agnostic about whether this intervention is effective in terms of reducing risk-taking and bank failures.

Changing bank behavior is one thing. But it is a very different question whether the regulatory intervention was effective in changing bank behavior in a way that reduced the number of bank failures, reduced the losses to the deposit insurance fund, or reduced the risk-taking at troubled banks—although I believe that to the extent intermediaries did make second bets, it was more a savings and loan than a commercial bank phenomenon.

Early intervention assumes that if the problem is caught early and the bank alters its behavior, it may be possible to reverse the bank's decline. However, to date, little definitive empirical evidence on this point has been produced. Such evidence is very important, insofar as we need to know the extent to which a trade-off exists between the costs to bank loan customers due to bank shrinkage and the benefits to the FDIC (and hence taxpayers) of reduced costs of bank failures. It is possible that bank survival is determined primarily by economic factors unrelated to regulatory intervention, in which case the shrinkage of bank assets in response to regulatory actions may have little or no effect on the probability of a bank's survival. As the authors acknowledge, while the recovery of many banks is consistent with positive results from regulatory intervention, we cannot be sure about the extent to which any recovery in bank health can be attributed to management, stockholders, market forces, or bank supervisors.

With the information that we have available, we cannot yet distinguish whether the bank shrinkage that resulted from regulatory intervention was analogous to sending in the leeches for a round of bloodletting—an analogy that many bankers may find appealing—or did, in fact, cause banks to take on less risk and get their houses in order. Certainly, when it comes time to shrink, troubled assets are the least marketable, so one could imagine that the shrinkage occurs disproportionately through the sale of the better-quality assets that can fetch a price closer to book value. Consequently, the remaining portfolio may be more, rather than less, risky.

In terms of prompt corrective action, we can answer the question of whether intervention has been prompt. But we are still some distance away from being able to answer the question of whether intervention has been corrective. However, the construction of the expanded panel data set that is the heart of the "History of the Eighties" project will greatly increase the range of regulatory actions and bank reactions that can be examined carefully and in depth. The resulting research should provide an empirical basis for understanding the impact of intervention provisions such as those in FDICIA, enabling policymakers to make much more precise inferences about how different types of bank regulation affect both bank behavior and performance.

The role of regulatory intervention has been largely ignored in most failure studies. We need to look not only at those banks that failed, but at those that recovered, and see if we can develop an understanding of those factors that contributed to their recovery. Did those banks recover because of supervisory intervention, or in spite of the intervention? Does recovery depend on initial conditions, for example, the bank's health at the time of the formal regulatory action? Thus, how important is the promptness of the intervention and the speed at which the bank's health is deteriorating? Is there a point of no return and, if so, what is it? Is it really a 2 percent tangible capital ratio? Do differences in bank reactions to supervisory intervention really make a difference? What role do local economic conditions play in the probability of a troubled bank recovering? What it comes down to is this: Once a bank is identified as troubled, is there still time, and a method, to reduce its probability of failure by a meaningful amount?

Conclusion and Recommendations

Bank regulatory policies have been proposed, enacted, and implemented with laudable intentions, but little clear understanding of their positive or negative consequences. To some degree, regulatory legislation and policy have been based on economic theory, and even more often, on economic theology, assumptions, guesses, and wishful thinking; but rarely have they been based on solid evidence—because the evidence was not available. This omission was a direct consequence of our failure to construct a comprehensive database with which we could ask, and answer with confidence, the important questions concerning how regulatory intervention works, whether it accomplishes what is intended, and how it can be made more effective. That such a database had not been constructed is not particularly surprising when one thinks about the focus of examiners, the ones with the data; they are interested in today and tomorrow, not the past. Only research economists have the luxury of sitting back and doing retrospective studies.

To design and implement sensible regulatory policies, we need to learn the extent to which our good intentions have, in fact, become outcomes. The "History of the Eighties" project is an important first step in providing the evidence that can make regulatory intervention and policy more effective, but it is only a first step. We need to continue these efforts to provide a comprehensive database with which researchers can carefully investigate the role and consequences of regulatory policy. And we must continue to encourage the commingling of examiner and research resources. The whole is far greater than the sum of the parts.

References

Peek, Joe and Eric S. Rosengren. 1995. "Banks and the Availability of Small Business Loans," Federal Reserve Bank of Boston Working Paper No. 95-1, January.

————. 1996. "The Use of Capital Ratios to Trigger Intervention in Problem Banks: Too Little, Too Late," *New England Economic Review*, September/October, pp. 49-58.

————. 1997. "Will Legislated Early Intervention Prevent the Next Banking Crisis?" *Southern Economic Review*, July, forthcoming.

Comments on Bank Examination and Enforcement
Stephen R. Steinbrink*

I find myself largely in agreement with the lessons of the eighties that are in the study, but would like to make several comments regarding them. Then I will move on to discuss some other issues that I believe might be important as the regulatory agencies go forward. Now that I have retired and it won't seem self-serving, I do want to mention that the regulatory agencies have a very difficult job, particularly from the standpoint that it is a given that they are going to be criticized regardless of what they do. So, they might just as well be happy being criticized.

The first lesson of the eighties that was listed in the paper was that reduction in resources didn't work. A few points should be added to that general statement. First, you need to realize that the reduction of resources occurred during a period when the number and the size of the institutions were expanding dramatically. My experience in this area during this time was almost entirely in the Southwest District of the Office of the Comptroller of the Currency. It should be pointed out that there was never a policy in the Comptroller's office to reduce the number of resources in the Southwest District. There were, however, reductions due to circumstances. The District had over a 20 percent turnover rate, and there were nationwide hiring freezes as a result of the administration's desire to reduce government in general. These circumstances thrust the Southwest District—when the hiring freezes were in effect— into having to hire very carefully to try to bring on just enough staff so that there were experienced examiners to train them and still accomplish on-site examinations during the time. It should be noted that almost all examiner training is on-site in the bank and not in the classroom.

Because of that reduction in resources, there were fewer examinations and a less experienced staff; there is no doubt that this hindered the identification of problem banks. At present, however, if you were to look at the statistics (though I have been gone from the OCC almost a year now), I believe almost 80 percent of the staff of the OCC consists of Commissioned National Bank Examiners, which means that they have been on the job approximately five years, and probably more than five years. So, there is now a lot of experience in the regulatory agencies.

* The author was Senior Deputy Comptroller of the Currency for Bank Supervision, Office of the Comptroller of the Currency, from March 1993 to May 1996 and from July 1991 to February 1992.

I would nominate as a second lesson, that there has to be some effort to merge "economic information" and "examiner information" within the examination process. All the agencies have tried this for some time, but with only limited overall success. Let us consider an example of why this would be important. If you were a bank examiner in Texas in the 1980s, and you went to a board of directors to discuss problems in real estate that had not yet been specifically identified (in other words, it was possible to see concentrations and potential for problems in the future), it was likely that half of that board consisted of real estate developers. They were not going to believe you when you said that their industry was heading down a path that perhaps they ought to step back and assess. If you could have gone to them with some sort of economic information, along with your examining skills, then you would have had a much better chance of changing their minds or perhaps getting them to be thoughtful about the process. You would hopefully have been more effective in that regard. It strikes me that if we do not do that, all the examiners and all the examinations are probably for naught. We must give the examiners the skills to have an impact on what is affecting those banks day-in, day-out in their operations and in their competition. I believe this is a crucial point. All the regulators right now are working on doing this, although they are using different methods, and are having different levels of success.

I will certainly agree that on-site examinations are extremely important. Off-site examinations are also very beneficial. During interim periods, they can increase the efficiency of the process. They can assist in the scheduling and conducting of exams. But despite all that, it remains necessary to go into the institution and look somebody in the eye and discuss the problems that exist in the bank, or even just to ask a question and evaluate the response. There are also some very practical reasons for on-site examinations, particularly in small institutions. First, a small institution is paying something and they deserve something back. Second, some of the small institutions actually consider the examination important as a third-party view of their work. Finally, the fact of the matter is that the simple presence of an examiner serves as a discipline and that is beneficial to the process.

With regard to the rating systems, the agencies have wanted to make those systems forward-looking. We have tried and tried and, to be honest, haven't been very successful at it. There have been isolated instances where the ratings systems have been forward-looking, but those have been very few. I believe, however, that within the last year, each of the regulatory agencies has discussed a process that while it did not involve new rating systems, did result in supplements to the rating system, and that is the new discussion of risk. I think that is in response to the lessons learned in the 1980s, at least to some extent. In the Comptroller of the Currency's risk management publications, there is actually reference to assessing the direction of risk, which I believe directly addresses the concern regarding looking forward, and that is identifying where the risk is headed and looking toward the future. I guess the vote will still be out as to whether that ends up being successful. I know before I left, and I'm sure it is still going on, that everybody is working on that.

As to enforcement actions, the paper indicates, given what was studied, that there was not a large distinction between formal and informal actions as to what happened to improve the conditions of the institutions. I am not sure that I agree with that conclusion, but do not have any real basis for disagreeing with it. The point I would make about enforcement actions, and in some respects this agrees with the paper, is that the document is not nearly as important as the presentation of the document by the regulatory agency, because when you present the document to the bank, your goal is to get their attention. In most cases, the bankers go through a period of denial where they believe that the regulator is just not seeing the institution in the right light. If you are effective in presenting the facts, then you get the bank and the board's attention. The bank and board take action—sometimes immediately—to deal with whatever problems exist. I am not talking about banks that are going to fail in a week. But, if you are dealing with a bank that has a problem that could lead to potential failure two years later and you get their attention and they take immediate action, when you go to the bank 3-4 months afterward with a document, everybody will sign it, but will also indicate that they have already taken action.

The fact is, that if the examiner, at least at the OCC, is doing his or her job properly, then the day they leave the bank, the day they have an exit meeting, they should have told that institution everything that will be in the document when it finally comes. If the bank accepts that fact and starts action, then by the time the supervisors get the document processed, you are presumably a long way down the road toward corrective action. However, there are many times you just do not get corrective action. I was disappointed that the OCC's enforcement actions were not given to the authors of the study, but while I don't have the statistics in front of me, if my recollection serves me properly, at one point I think about 80 percent of all national banks in the United States had some sort of action, and probably at least half of those were formal.

The next to last issue I wanted to mention was Prompt Corrective Action (PCA), about which there has been much debate. Some like it; some do not; I am ambivalent. One former chairman of the FDIC made the statement that there will come a time when we could regret the regulatory agencies having been put in a position of having to close banks that did not need to fail. I can see that argument, but I would temper that statement just slightly. In my experience with the large bank population, and I don't know if this was the intent of PCA, but when FDICIA was implemented and the capital ratios were finally established, managements and boards immediately began to take action to ensure that their institutions would never be affected by PCA. Now, regulators always like to take credit for things but we did not have a thing to do with that action. The reason those capital relationships went up was only because they didn't want their stock to be affected by their capital proximity to PCA. It was driven totally by their worry about the stock market and Wall Street. They therefore raised capital, and that is probably a good thing. Overall, I do not believe that PCA was a bad law, although some of its provisions are a little draconian. As a practical matter, however, if you go back and look at the enforcement documents, there is nothing in PCA that isn't in most of them, perhaps with the exception of the removal of directors, which was not a common practice.

Finally, in the paper there is a reference to the delay in the closure of banks. I am always sensitive to that because a lot of them were OCC banks. When you look at how long it took to close a bank and you look to the comparison of PCA, it is very important to remember a regulation—because of the definitions of capital, the OCC, until year-end 1989, had to charge off every dollar of capital and every dollar of the allowance for loan and lease losses before a bank could be declared insolvent. This had a dramatic impact on national banks, because many states had a different capital definition whereby they could close a bank based on viability. This regulation had a significant impact on the OCC.

In addition, I should note that I participated in establishing a very elaborate process for reviewing banks that were going to be declared insolvent. Examiners would perform the examination, would come up with losses, and would preliminarily find the bank insolvent. Then the line sheets were brought into the District office, just to be certain that they were correct. If it was a sufficiently significant bank, they might have been brought to the Washington office. I personally sat down and reviewed line sheets when I was the Senior Deputy Controller because I always thought that closing a bank was a really important issue. When you have sat down with a board of directors and closed a bank, you can see the impact it has on the individuals sitting in that room, who sometimes have their entire net worth wrapped up in that bank stock. I wanted to make damn sure that we did it right.

Panel 2

Off-Site
Surveillance Systems

Robert B. Avery
Mark J. Flannery

Off-Site Surveillance Systems

Off-Site Surveillance Systems in the 1980s and Lessons for the Future
Robert B. Avery*

Let me begin my discussion by commending the FDIC and its staff for preparing the studies presented as part of this symposium. These represent an extraordinary effort on their part to provide a retrospective evaluation of banking supervision and regulation in the 1980s. The papers present a lot of information that has heretofore not been made public. As one who continually struggles with making sense of bank Call Report data I realize how difficult it is to cull meaningful conclusions from inherently noisy and idiosyncratic data. They are to be commended on their efforts. These are extremely useful and interesting studies.

I want to focus my remarks on two broad questions: (1) what is the purpose of off-site monitoring? and (2) what lessons can be learned from the past 15 years that can be used to improve off-site monitoring in the future? Let me begin with the first question.

The FDIC staff study on off-site monitoring focuses most of its attention on evaluating the success of off-site methods in forecasting long-term bank failure. They examine the ability of statistical models based primarily on Call Report data to forecast bank failure (or problem bank status) two to five years in the future, basing their models on the experience of the 1980s. The models they test are not the models that were actually in place at the time, but ones that have been estimated subsequently. Their evaluation suggests that these models are likely to have

---

* The author is a senior economist in the Division of Research and Statistics at the Board of Governors of the Federal Reserve System. The views stated are those of the author and not necessarily those of the Board of Governors of the Federal Reserve System.

very limited success; that for every bank correctly forecast as failing in five years we will have eight to 14 that are forecast to fail but don't. I think that is a pretty good indication of the limits of the capability of such models. Augmented with local economic information (as the FDIC is currently initiating), I suspect we can do marginally better. But we are still likely to have substantial "type two" errors, or banks that are forecast to fail and don't.

Does this indicate that off-site long-term forecasting has limited value? Not necessarily, but only if we are willing to act on the basis of long-term forecasts and to tolerate substantial type two errors. That is, if we identify banks that have a higher risk for failure in five years, but are currently solvent, would we be willing to enforce changes in their behavior—to make them hold more capital or make other changes? If regulators are not willing to do that, then there is a real question as to whether or not we should be devoting resources to identifying those banks, even with low type two error rates. In other words, unless we actually act on the information we collect or gather, it may not be worth devoting a lot of time to such an effort.

There is also a question about whether long-term forecasting need be done exclusively off-site. Examination data can be tailored to this objective. Indeed, the new "risk evaluation" procedures are a step in this direction. Long-term forecasting is probably best done combining statistical and examination inputs.

Long-term forecasting needn't be the sole or primary purpose of off-site monitoring. The FDIC staff study also discusses the success of the banking agencies' models used to evaluate each new Call Report filing. These "short run" off-site models sift the data in a number of ways, such as comparisons within peer groups, in an attempt to identify those banks that appear to be reporting a material change in their condition since the previous Call Report or the previous exam. Although the staff study does not spend as much time evaluating success in this area as in long-term forecasting, my casual sense is that the short-run agency models do a pretty good job. It is unlikely that a bank would report a large material change in its Call Report and not get flagged.

The development of off-site monitoring methods has probably suffered because of an ambiguity about whether their purpose is long- or short-run forecasting. If the purpose of such methods is to forecast which banks will fail next year or have CAMEL downgrades, then the models should probably be built around identifying which banks are similar to other banks failing right now or currently being downgraded. On the other hand, long-run forecasting models are likely to be based more on fundamentals and needn't be continually re-estimated. The information that one would need to address these two objectives is potentially different, and would not necessarily be jointly produced by the same data-gathering system.

There is clearly a need to clarify the primary purpose of off-site monitoring. The answer probably lies in one's faith in the examination system. If one believes that on-site exams provide the most useful and accurate forecasts of long-term bank health, then the purpose of off-site monitoring would likely be seen as complementary to the exam system and very short-run in nature. On the other hand, if exams are thought to be useful primarily in assessing the current condition of a bank, then it might be appropriate to use off-site methods for long-term forecasts. Here, though, the issue of the willingness to act on this information needs to be broached.

I believe that the strongest case for off-site monitoring can be made for short-run forecasting. In an era when federal examiners may visit a bank only once in three years there is a strong need to develop methods to monitor banks between exams. In the remainder of my remarks I want to focus on ways that such a short-run forecasting tool might be improved and what issues need to be addressed before improvements could be made.

The first issue is, what information should be used? Current models are based primarily on Call Report data. This ignores a host of other data sources. These would include: local economic data; data from the previous exam of the bank; data from exams of similar banks; and, data collected from the bank itself, such as internal risk reports; data from market observers, such as prices of the bank's bonds and equity. One obvious question is should these alternative information sources be used, and if so, how?

A second issue is, what structure should off-site monitoring have? Should it be centralized? Done regionally? Or, should it be the responsibility of local examiners? Should the monitoring process differ by the size of bank or institutional structure? Should individual bank activities be separately monitored or should the focus be on monitoring the overall health of the bank?

A potential guide in answering these questions may come from looking at how banks monitor their credits. Banks have very much the same monitoring problem as bank regulators. The Call Report we receive from banks is very similar to the periodic balance-sheet data banks require their borrowers to supply. Yet, clearly banks require more from their borrowers; indeed examiners would severely criticize a bank that only looked at balance-sheet data. Even if the bank developed elaborate models that worked with balance-sheet data, if that was all that they did it would be viewed as inadequate. Banks require from borrowers more information than just balance sheet data. Examiners also expect banks to independently validate information obtained from borrowers through appraisals or independent evaluations.

Another important feature of bank monitoring systems is that they differ across loan and borrower types. A commercial real estate loan will be monitored differently from an inventory loan. Banks will seek different information from these two types of borrowers. The amount of effort expended on monitoring will also differ across credits. A lot less time will be spent monitoring a loan 100 percent collateralized by a bank CD than loans to borrowers entering Chapter 11.

Also, bank off-site monitoring systems tend to be decentralized. Information such as tax reports and balance-sheet data may be gathered centrally, but the ultimate responsibility for oversight is likely to lie primarily with individual loan officers.

Lastly, and perhaps most importantly, bank monitoring is forward-looking. Banks ask questions about what might happen to a creditor. They want early indicators of credits having problems. They don't necessarily wait until a credit is nonperforming before they start serious oversight.

A number of these features of bank monitoring systems would appear to offer potential improvements to the process of off-site regulatory bank monitoring. Perhaps the most compelling case can be made for making regulatory exams also forward looking. When an examiner completes an exam, they should be asked: In what areas is this bank most vulnerable to risk? What information would be most useful to have between exams in assessing this bank's health? What signals would most likely indicate a downturn in this bank's condition? My suspicion is that the answers that examiners would give to these questions would differ from bank to bank, and their information requests would almost surely not be restricted to Call Report data.

Another potential lesson we might learn from the banks is to decentralize; to assign examiners specific responsibility for off-site monitoring between exams. My own agency is moving in this direction, and similar efforts are afoot at the other agencies. Clearly, unless someone has the specific responsibility to monitor each bank, information is likely to fall between the cracks.

Another lesson that might be learned from banks is to utilize information gleaned from the oversight of one credit (or bank) in the monitoring of others. Bank exams tend to be done in isolation. Arguably some information does get disseminated, but channels of communication tend to be ad hoc and are particularly weak across agencies. There may be great value in sharing exam results, particularly if exam information can be systematized. The development of a joint examiner workstation just agreed to by the FDIC and Federal Reserve holds great promise for moving in this direction. Not only will the work station systematize exam reporting, but it also will allow the direct processing of individual bank loan data. If banks supplied loan files on a periodic basis between exams, it would allow us to detect changes in performance by industry and loan type. Internal bank ratings would also give clues as to changes in bank underwriting standards. There are many ways that such information could be utilized to vastly improve our off-site surveillance.

Alternative data sources also need to be developed. The FDIC's new Division of Insurance is moving in this direction. Such information can range from the macro, such as DRI forecasts, to the very localized, such as real estate reports on specific markets. We also need to rethink the information we obtain from banks. We could ask banks to fill out supplementary reports between exams that address items of specific relevance to that bank. These needn't be the same for each bank and could be tailored to their own situation.

In sum, I believe that there are a number of ways that off-site bank monitoring can be improved. None of these are likely to come to fruition, however, unless off-site monitoring is made an agency priority. It isn't enough to simply ask examiners to keep an eye on banks between exams or to compute a variety of peer group comparisons with Call Report data. We need to make it an area of focus for those in the policymaking parts of our agencies. We need to ask if we are supplying examiners and other off-site monitors with the tools and information with which to do their job. I think these are all areas in which we have much to learn and where there is much room for improvement.

Off-Site Surveillance Systems

Mark J. Flannery*

Jack Reidhill and John O'Keefe (FDIC [1997]) have provided an extensive review of the issues associated with off-site supervision for U.S. commercial banks. I am impressed—even awed—by the informational detail underlying their analysis, and join the earlier speakers in congratulating the FDIC on its retrospective evaluation of this important, but not always flattering, decade in our financial history.

I would like to begin my discussion by presenting a schematic interpretation of the main concern in this paper. Figure 1 summarizes the process of identifying a problem bank and producing a regulatory response. The first relevant date is when the bank initiates the policies that will eventually place it in danger of failing. While this event passes unnoticed at the time, regulatory oversight seeks to identify such changes in bank condition or risk exposure as soon as possible.

Suppose a system of on-site examinations would identify the bank's increased failure probability at the point B. We can describe the time from 0 to B as the exam system's *Recognition Lag*. Anecdotal evidence strongly suggests that examiners and their supervisors cannot usually impose corrective action at B, but must wait until subsequent developments have made it obvious that the bank has a real problem. Call this interval the *Action Lag*.[1] Reidhill and O'Keefe's paper extensively discusses whether off-site statistical modeling of banks' quarterly Report of Condition data could shorten the Recognition Lag from [0, B] to [0, A], and this is an important question. However, policymakers should primarily be

Figure 1

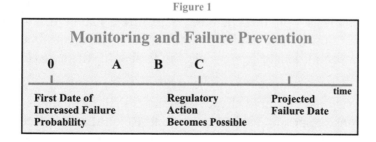

Monitoring and Failure Prevention

| 0 | A | B | C | | |

| First Date of Increased Failure Probability | | Regulatory Action Becomes Possible | Projected Failure Date | time |

---

* The author is Barnett Banks Professor of Finance at the University of Florida.

[1] The Action Lag may reflect administrative delays within the agency, or examiners' reluctance to impose costly oversight on a bank while its accounting condition remains "good."

concerned with the *sum* of the Recognition and Action Lags. Unless supervisors can implement corrective actions earlier than time C, the gains from shortening the Recognition Lag seem limited.

Reidhill and O'Keefe provide extensive analysis of several off-site monitoring systems (GMS, CAEL, FIMS) in terms of a loss function that values the number of Type I and Type II errors. Rather than evaluating the *number* of banks that are correctly identified, I would aim for a system that correctly identifies the largest proportion of problem bank *assets*. The best system for forecasting the *average* bank's problems is unlikely to be optimal for forecasting the *largest* banks' problems. Given that the costs of bank failures are (at least) proportional to the bank's size, we should reconsider the paper's equally-weighted objective function for evaluating off-site surveillance systems.

Still another question raised by Reidhill and O'Keefe (FDIC [1997]) concerns the role of on-site examinations in ensuring the accuracy of Report of Condition data. Gilbert (1993) argues that on-site bank exams materially improve the accuracy of Report of Condition data. Dahl, Hanweck, and O'Keefe (1995) find that examiners more effectively force managers to recognize loan losses than auditors do. An important question remains, however, whether private auditors could be induced to provide effective oversight in this regard. Would this be a cheaper means of producing accurate data?

These three points are little more than quibbles about a basically informative analysis of the FDIC's supervisory efforts. The main issue I would like to discuss concerns not what the paper says, but rather what it does *not* say. I was surprised and disappointed to find no mention of a vast source of skilled workers whose talents could arguably be used to the advantage of federal bank supervisors. What is more, these analysts' opinions could be had for free! The FDIC's apparent failure to recognize this off-site source of opinion and judgment about individual banks' financial conditions disquiets me, as it should all taxpayers and bank creditors.

The analysts I have in mind already customize their evaluations to reflect the varying situations of specific banks—something Reidhill and O'Keefe point out that statistical models have not done very well. Moreover, these analysts intensify their efforts when economic conditions make it most difficult to understand the condition of financial firms: when macroeconomic conditions are less predictable, or in geographic areas threatened or beset by regional recession. These analysts are, of course, market investors and their advisers: rating agencies, stock analysts, brokers, and investment underwriters.

The FDIC's internal efforts to predict bank problems do not exist in a vacuum. Many private analysts grapple daily with the same problem, and their conclusions get reflected in bank security prices, bond ratings, institutional portfolio compositions, bank insiders' portfolio holdings, and so forth. An important policy issue concerns whether federal regulators could systematically use some of this market information to complement their own methods of identifying changes in bank condition or risk exposure. I am not suggesting that supervisors casually "look at" market data, which they clearly do for at least the largest banks. Rather, I propose that a formal integration of selected market data into the regulatory agencies' analytical systems could substantially improve the quality of the oversight they can provide.

I hope to convince you today that this question warrants serious, substantial investigation.

A. "If You Build It, They Will Come ..."

Some preliminary evidence that bank debenture-holders can identify bank risk exposures is provided in Flannery and Sorescu (1996). We collected yield data on all fixed-rate bank debentures outstanding during the period 1983–1991, and computed option-adjusted spreads over Treasury (SPREAD) as proxies for the market's assessment of individual bank failure probabilities.[2] Recall that Continental Illinois' crisis occurred during the summer of 1984, and precipitated the Comptroller's "too big to fail" testimony before Congress that September. The TBTF policy *de facto* applied to bank debentures until the late 1980s, when pressures on the bank insurance fund led regulators to impose losses on debenture-holders in an increasing number of problem bank resolutions.

Figure 2 plots the mean (median) value of our sample's risk premium at each year-end in the sample period. Until 1989, the typical debenture SPREAD is relatively small, but it rises sharply once debenture-holders become exposed to default losses. Similarly, Figure 3 reveals that the cross-sectional variation in SPREAD (measured as its standard deviation or the inter-quartile range) also rose after 1988.

---

[2] Avery, Belton and Goldberg (1988) and Gorton and Santomero (1990) previously evaluated the determinants of debenture risk premia for the relatively quiescent 1983–84 period.

Figure 2

Option-Adjusted SPREADs on Subordinated Debentures

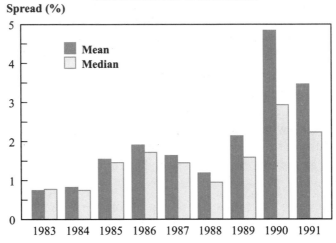

Spread (%)

Figure 3

Cross-Sectional Variability in SPREAD

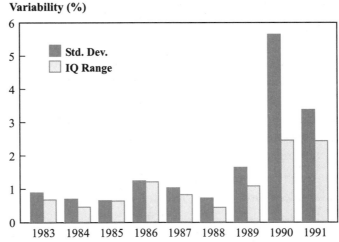

Variability (%)

B. Do Sufficient Market Data Exist?

When the question arises whether market-based information could supplement the regulatory agencies' traditional methods, I frequently encounter two practical objections.

1. Market data are unavailable for the vast majority of U.S. banks.

2. Market assessments of a bank's condition are likely to be inferior and out-of-date, because on-site examinations uncover important inside information that outsiders cannot obtain.

I contend that the first objection is not materially correct, and that the second one has never been seriously tested.

Market Data Exist for Firms Controlling the Majority of Banking Assets

While the majority of U.S. banking companies do not have publicly traded stock or bonds, this is not true for the majority of banking system *assets*. M. Nimalendran, Simon Kwan, and I (1997) have recently assembled an extensive data set for banks with publicly traded stock.[3] Coverage of the banking system for the third quarter of 1995 is illustrated in Table 1. We find that more than 15 percent of all banks are associated with holding companies whose equity shares trade on the NYSE, AMEX, or NASDAQ exchanges. More importantly, these 1,599 banks hold more than three trillion dollars in assets, comprising fully three-quarters of the U.S. banking system. Despite the fact that most banks by number have no traded equity, the banks that collectively pose the most important challenge to federal regulators' supervisory abilities are not included in that group. The fact that

Table 1

Market Data Availability for U.S. Banking Firms

Sample of 344 bank holding companies with traded equity shares as of September 30, 1995.
(data from Flannery, Kwan, and Nimalendran [1997])

Primary Regulator	Number of Banks	Percentage of all U.S. Banks	Bank Assets	Percentage of U.S. Bank Assets
OCC	639	6.2%	$1,866 billion	45.1%
Federal Reserve	246	2.4%	$ 828 billion	20.0%
FDIC	590	5.7%	$ 336 billion	8.1%
Other (e.g. Edge)	124	1.2%	$ 69 billion	1.7%
Total	1599	**15.4%**	$3,099 billion	**75.0%**

---

[3] I am grateful to Simon Kwan for providing the numbers in Table 1.

market data are not available for many banks does not justify ignoring them for the largest banking firms, which control 75 percent of all U.S. banking assets.

Are Private Assessments Lagging Indicators of Bank Quality?

Hard information on the relative timeliness of private vs. government information about bank quality is difficult to obtain, in large part because the regulatory agencies have generally been unwilling to share their quality assessments with academic researchers.[4] Two Federal Reserve Board economists and I have collaborated on a research project that compares public and regulatory assessments of bank holding company condition (Berger, Davies, and Flannery [1997]). For a sample of about 180 large bank holding companies, we gathered quarterly data on market assessments of bank condition:

1. abnormal stock return,

2. proportion of common equity shares held by insiders,

3. proportion of common equity shares held by institutional (13-F) investors, and

4. the Moody's rating on outstanding debentures.

We matched these data with BOPEC ratings, the dates of on-site holding company inspections, and accounting (Y-9) information over the period 1988–1992.[5]

As one part of our analysis, Berger, Davies, and I evaluated whether market or regulatory agents could better predict future changes in three key indicators of bank condition: the fraction of outstanding loans that were nonperforming, the return on assets, and the equity capital ratio. Specifically, we regressed each bank variable on lagged values of our market assessments of bank condition, the lagged BOPEC rating, lagged dummies for the existence of an on-site examination, and lagged values of the bank's accounting ratios. If the Fed has superior information about BHC condition, we should find that BOPEC ratings change before market assessments do, and that on-site inspections tend to be scheduled before accounting data indicate potential problems.

---

[4] Regulators have been reluctant to disclose current CAMEL ratings, for example, because they fear that publication of any negative assessments could become self-fulfilling prophesies, causing the affected banks to suffer even greater difficulties. While the potential publication of current CAMEL ratings raises a host of difficult questions, providing historical ratings to disinterested researchers under a pledge of confidentiality seems less problematic.

[5] In order to ensure the confidentiality of BOPEC ratings, I was not permitted to see the raw data, but only the results of our analysis and tests, which were undertaken at the Federal Reserve Board.

The qualitative results are reported in Figures 4–6. Each figure identifies the statistically significant coefficients on lagged assessments. Rather than reporting the (relatively meaningless) coefficient values themselves, I show the proportion of the cumulative lagged effect that occurs in each quarter.

Figure 4a shows several important points about the ability of market variables to predict changes in reported ROA.

1. The BHC's abnormal stock return rises (falls) significantly one and three quarters prior to an increase (decline) in reported ROA.

2. Officers and directors change the proportion of outstanding stock in their own portfolios in each of the second, third, and fourth quarters preceding the change in ROA.

3. Institutional holdings of a BHC's stock show no change in anticipation of a change in reported ROA.

In sum, two observable market assessments of bank quality seem to predict changes in ROA.

How about regulatory assessments? These are illustrated in Figure 4b. BOPEC DN and BOPEC UP are dummy variables equal to unity if the BOPEC rating was lowered or raised (respectively) during the calendar quarter.[6] EXAM is a dummy variable equal to unity if an on-site holding company inspection occurred during the quarter. Figure 4b indicates that only BOPEC *reductions* significantly lead changes in ROA, by one and two quarters. We find no evidence that BOPEC improvements or on-site inspections systematically precede a change in ROA.

Figures 5a and 5b report results for changes in bank NPL ratios—the ratio of nonperforming loans to total loans outstanding. Abnormal stock returns lead dNPL by one and two quarters, while insiders' and institutions' shareholdings both lead changes in NPL by two and four quarters. By contrast, EXAM has a small predictive effect at quarters t-1 and t-2, while BOPEC DN exhibits (puzzling) offsetting effects in quarters t-2 and t-3. Once again, our results indicate

---

[6] The cardinal scaling of BOPEC ratings—with "1" being "best" and "5" being "worst"—inevitably creates semantic difficulties. We interpret BOPEC UP to mean an improvement in the firm's condition—e.g., a change from BOPEC=3 to BOPEC=2.

Figure 4a
dROA After Changes in Market Variables
(Only Significant Effects Shown)

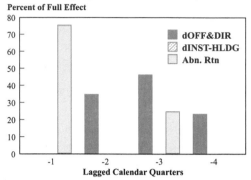

Figure 4b
dROA After Changes in Regulatory Variables
(Only Significant Effects Shown)

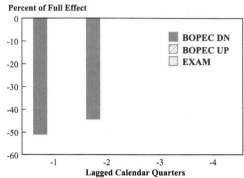

Figure 5a
dNPL After Changes in Market Variables
(Only Significant Effects Shown)

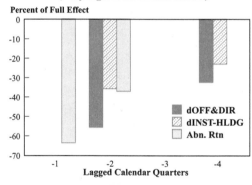

Figure 5b
dNPL After Changes in Regulatory Variables
(Only Significant Effects Shown)

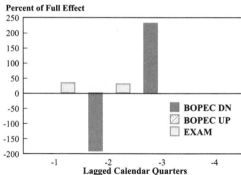

Figure 6a
dCAPITAL After Changes in Market Variables
(Only Significant Effects Shown)

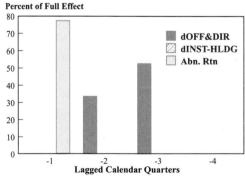

Figure 6b
dCAPITAL After Changes in Regulatory Variables
(Only Significant Effects Shown)

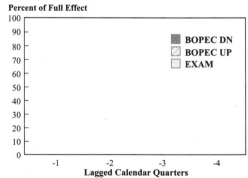

that market assessments of bank condition are, if anything, more predictive of changes in bank condition.

Figures 6a and 6b present similar results for changes in a bank's CAPITAL ratio (book value of equity capital divided by total assets). A high abnormal stock return tends to predict higher CAPITAL in the subsequent quarter, while the insiders' shareholdings lead changes in CAPITAL by two and three quarters. In contrast, Figure 6b shows that *none* of our regulatory variables significantly predicts changes in CAPITAL.

Taken all together, the results in Figures 4–6 suggest that market assessments of bank condition *do not* lag behind regulatory assessments. If anything, the converse appears to hold. One possibility consistent with these findings is that BOPEC ratings are not generally revised without an on-site inspection, and these inspections take time to schedule and implement. Our data cannot rule out the possibility that regulators "knew" of changes in a bank's condition, but chose to postpone formally changing the BOPEC. This possibility raises several further questions about the true meaning of BOPEC (or CAMEL) ratings. However, my basic point is that market assessments appear to have at least a plausible chance of providing timely, accurate information that supplements the supervisory agencies' traditional ways of gathering and assessing information about bank quality.

C. Conclusion

Market signals about bank quality are available for much of the banking industry, though we have no conclusive evidence that markets provide the most useful information available about traded bank holding companies and their subsidiaries. Only a substantial research program can determine whether or how market information may complement supervisors' current procedures. This research must recognize that the presence and quality of market signals vary with creditors' perceived exposure to default risk. Because failure resolution policies blunted market incentives for much of the 1980s, we must interpret empirical evidence from that period—when we had our greatest number of large bank failures—with great care. I do believe, however, that the data and research I have described this morning suggest that the market assessments of banks warrant serious consideration within the regulatory agencies.

References

Avery, Robert B., Terrence M. Belton, and Michael A. Goldberg. "Market Discipline in Regulating Bank Risk: New Evidence from the Capital Markets." *Journal of Money, Credit and Banking* 20, no. 4 (1988), pp. 597-610.

Berger, Allen N., Sally M. Davies, and Mark J. Flannery. "Comparing Market and Regulatory Assessments of Bank Performance: Who Knows What When?" mimeo (February 1997).

Dahl, Drew, Gerald A. Hanweck, and John O'Keefe. "The Influence of Auditors and Examiners on Accounting Discretion in the Banking Industry." FDIC Working Paper (October 1995).

Federal Deposit Insurance Corporation. "Off-Site Surveillance Systems in the 1980s and Early 1990s. " Draft (December 1996) of Chapter 13 in Federal Deposit Insurance Corporation, *History of the Eighties—Lessons for the Future*, Vol. 1 (1997).

Flannery, Mark J. and Sorin M. Sorescu. "Evidence of Bank Market Discipline in Subordinated Debenture Yields: 1983–1991." *Journal of Finance* (September 1996), pp. 1347-1377.

Flannery, Mark J., Simon H. Kwan, and M. Nimalendran. "Market Evidence on the Opaqueness of Banking Firms' Assets." mimeo (1997).

Gilbert, R. Alton. "Implications of Annual Examinations for the Bank Insurance Fund." Federal Reserve Bank of St. Louis *Review* 75, no. 1 (Jan.-Feb. 1993), pp. 35-52.

Gorton, Gary and Anthony M. Santomero. "Market Discipline and Bank Subordinated Debt." *Journal of Money, Credit and Banking* 22, no. 1 (1990), pp. 119-128.

Keynote Address

Ricki Helfer

Keynote Address

Remarks by Ricki Helfer, Chairman, Federal Deposit Insurance Corporation*

It has been said that experience is a tough teacher—first you get the test, then you learn the lesson. In the banking crisis of the 1980s and early 1990s, banking regulators were tested, and from their experience they learned lessons. Did we learn the correct lessons?

When I became FDIC Chairman, I initiated a project to find the answer to that question, an answer based on objective analysis. The result is a series of 13 papers we will publish over the coming year. The purpose of this symposium is to discuss the first three papers in this series, which focus on supervisory issues.

This afternoon, I want to focus my remarks on the role of Federal deposit insurance in our banking and financial system. One of the lessons of the 1980s and early 1990s is that deposit insurance was eminently successful in maintaining stability in the banking system during the crisis. A second lesson is that this success came at enormous cost to the insurance funds, to the taxpayer, to the surviving institutions, and to their customers.

Our experience in the crisis reminded us that guaranteeing savings can be a costly business, although it may be necessary to stabilize the banking system in times of stress to prevent runs on individual banks from spreading to become banking panics.

One event toward the end of the most recent banking crisis underscored how quickly public confidence can evaporate—and the importance of deposit insurance in maintaining public confidence in the banking system.

In early 1991—just six years ago—the *New York Times* described recent events at the Bank of New England in this way:

---

* Ricki Helfer left her position as Chairman of the FDIC in May 1997.

"Frantic depositors pulled nearly $1 billion out of the bank in two days; small savers trooped through the lobbies with their money in wallets, bulging envelopes and briefcases, and money managers yanked out multimillion-dollar deposits by remote control with computer and telex orders.

"Some local crooks even tried to get in on the action. The Federal Bureau of Investigation said it foiled a plan by six men who had hoped to rob an armored car they figured would be loaded with cash for all the withdrawals."

The *New York Times* story concluded: "Yet as soon as Washington stepped in, with the Federal Deposit Insurance Corporation taking over the bank on Sunday, the panic subsided."

Bank of New England customers may have had doubts about their bank—but their doubts were not contagious. Because Federal deposit insurance maintained public confidence in the banking system, a run on the Bank of New England did not spread to other banks or into a general banking panic, with depositors at other banks demanding their funds, too.

How costly was this protection?

From 1980 through 1994—1,617 banks failed or received financial assistance from the FDIC. These failures severely tested the FDIC insurance fund. During the same period, nearly 1,300 savings and loans failed. These failures more than bankrupted the old savings and loan insurance fund and directly cost the taxpayers of America $125 billion, and billions more in indirect costs.

As a result of the experience of the 1980s and early 1990s, deposit insurance has become part of the continuing debate on how the banking industry should be modernized—and at the center of the discussion of deposit insurance is the problem of moral hazard.

The problem of moral hazard occurs when insurance induces the insured to take more risk than they would take if they were not insured. Any deposit insurance fund—any form of insurance, in fact—faces the problem of moral hazard. With deposit insurance, the insured party is the depositor. Insurance permits insured depositors to ignore the condition of their institutions. Even fundamentally unsound institutions may have little difficulty obtaining funds. Because insured depositors may no longer have an incentive to monitor and discipline their institutions, the managers of those institutions may take more risks than they otherwise would. In short, deposit insurance can create opportunities for managers to make high risk/high return investments, without the market discipline of having to pay creditors to take that risk.

Moreover, as the paper that is the subject of the next panel states: "with respect to the basic tradeoff between promoting stability and controlling moral hazard, bank regulators (in the 1980s) showed a preference for solutions that tipped the balance toward stability, a policy that was apparent in the treatment of large-bank failures.

"This contributed to the success of the deposit insurance system in avoiding bank runs and disruptive interruptions in credit flows. . . . (But) By protecting uninsured depositors, the methods used to resolve large-bank failures removed a source of market discipline that could have reinforced supervisory efforts to constrain risk."

To inform the debate over deposit insurance in the context of modernizing the banking charter, today I want to ask a number of fundamental questions, beginning with a question based on our experience in the 1980s and 1990s.

Did the problem of moral hazard created by Federal deposit insurance lead to a large number of failures of insured institutions in the 1980s and early 1990s, causing massive losses in the insurance funds?

To answer that question, moral hazard has to be broken into two components. First, in the case of a solvent institution, deposit insurance may lessen— or may eliminate—the incentive for insured creditors to monitor the activities of management and owners. Second, where a banking organization is insolvent or is approaching insolvency, deposit insurance may provide an incentive to bank management to take abnormal risks, thus magnifying losses to the insurance fund.

For the thrift industry in the 1980s, moral hazard contributed to huge losses in the savings and loan insurance fund, to its ultimate failure, and to substantial costs to the taxpayer. What began as an asset/liability mismatch problem, aggravated by rapidly rising interest rates in the beginning of the decade, became an enormous credit problem as real estate markets collapsed.

Weak regulatory oversight and the lack of resources to close insolvent thrifts encouraged some institutions to speculate widely in real estate and other ill-conceived efforts to "grow" out of their problems.

For banks in the 1980s and early 1990s, the role that moral hazard played in the significant losses to the insurance fund is not as clear. Certainly, deposit insurance did remove the incentive for insured creditors to monitor a bank's activities, but its effect is difficult to measure.

Moreover, the moral hazard that arises when banks approached insolvency and owners had less and less at stake was effectively restrained to a much greater extent than was the case with savings and loans by supervision of problem institutions. As will be detailed this afternoon, this restraint is indicated by the dividend, capital, and asset growth behavior of problem banks at that time.

Higher prudential standards for banks and more immediate regulatory attention to serious problems—as well as a solvent bank insurance fund with the resources to solve problems as they were identified—accounted for the difference in the experience of banks and thrifts. This difference should inform the debate over the role of deposit insurance in banking's future.

As this debate has developed, two alternatives to the current system have been offered: The first is to privatize the deposit insurance system. The second is to reduce the scope of the current system, and thus rely more on the markets to discipline the banking system. The two alternatives are, of course, not mutually exclusive.

Let's briefly analyze these proposals by seeking answers to four questions: One, what led Congress to make deposit insurance the responsibility of the Federal government? Two, can deposit insurance effectively be provided by another supplier? Three, how much less than the equivalent of a "full faith and credit" pledge by the Federal government will the public accept? Four, would reducing the scope of the deposit insurance system bring positive results?

First, what led Congress to make deposit insurance the responsibility of the Federal government?

Recurring and worsening banking panics marked the history of banking in the United States until the creation of the Federal Deposit Insurance Corporation in 1933. Nine thousand banks suspended operations from 1930 through 1933. The year after the FDIC was created, nine insured banks failed.

Even though the banking crisis of the 1980s and early 1990s resulted in a dramatically high number of bank failures, there was no banking panic—no contagion that could have threatened sound banks—and public confidence in the banking system held steady.

Today the banking industry is healthy and the economy is strong. Because the memories in good times can be short, it is important to remember the lessons of history.

It was the historical experience in the 1930s that has led a broad range of economists to conclude that Federal deposit insurance solved a problem that had plagued the banking system—and the economy—for more than a century, the problem of maintaining public confidence in a banking system marked by liabilities that were liquid and assets that were illiquid.

For example, in his *The Great Crash, 1929*, John Kenneth Galbraith observed: "Federal insurance of bank deposits, even to this day, has not been given full credit for the revolution that it has worked in the nation's banking structure. With this one piece of legislation, the fear which operated so efficiently to transmit weakness was dissolved. As a result one grievous defect of the old system, by which failure begot failure, was cured. Rarely has so much been accomplished by a single law."

In their *A Monetary History of the United States, 1867-1960*, Milton Friedman and Anna J. Schwartz similarly laud the role of deposit insurance in stabilizing the banking system: "Federal insurance of bank deposits was the most important structural change in the banking system to result from the 1933 panic and, indeed in our view, the structural change most conducive to monetary stability since state banknote issues were taxed out of existence immediately after the Civil War."

More recently, Federal Reserve Board Governor Janet Yellen, who has been nominated to become Chairwoman of the Council of Economic Advisors, addressed the issue also by reminding us of history. She said: "Deposit insurance was introduced both to protect individual depositors and to prevent panics surrounding individual banks from spreading throughout the financial system.

"Would we be better off as a country giving that up?" Governor Yellen asked rhetorically. "I don't think it is obvious that we would be. We would have to think through very carefully what implications the reduction or elimination of deposit insurance would have for systemic risk. The Depression taught us a lesson."

These tributes to Federal deposit insurance, however, do not address the question of whether a supplier other than the Federal government can provide essential depositor protection. In answering that question, the experience of private and state insurance providers in the banking crisis of the 1980s and early 1990s should give us some guidance.

As recently as 1982, there were 32 deposit insurance funds in operation. Only eight survived the crisis. Six operate today, three cover state credit unions and three are very limited in scope or are being phased out. Almost all the other funds collapsed because of the failure of one or more institutions. Most of the funds were state-sponsored, although the state did not usually provide any financial guarantees to the fund. These funds typically were mutual insurance funds with a board of directors drawn from the insured institutions.

In response to the failure of state deposit insurance plans in Ohio and Maryland, those states required state-chartered institutions to obtain Federal deposit insurance. Approximately 150 institutions were added to FDIC coverage in 1985 as a result.

Federal Reserve Chairman Alan Greenspan has observed: "Confidence in the stability of the banking and payments system has been the major reason why the United States has not suffered a financial panic or systemic bank run in the last half century."

It is my belief that deposit insurance can help maintain stability in the banking system only if depositors have confidence in the insurance plan. To inspire confidence during a period of turmoil, deposit insurance must be a certainty for the insured depositor.

The experience with private and state-sponsored insurance plans in the 1980s and early 1990s suggests that the limited pool of resources on which they can draw inspires less confidence than does the unlimited pool of resources of the Federal government. Bank failures may come in waves, because the performance of the industry is closely tied to the performance of the economy.

While it may be possible to design private insurance funds that could handle isolated failures successfully, our experience in the 1980s in Ohio and in Maryland suggests that limited plans have difficulty handling failures in waves.

Further, if private insurance is substituted for Federal deposit insurance, a private insurance plan facing depletion of its fund during a crisis would likely have to seek financing from the banking industry or other private sources of funds at the same time that the economy may be weak and the banking industry is having difficulties. Moreover, if the private insurance supplier fails, the Congress may have to act to restore public confidence. That would take time, and based upon the experience during the savings and loan crisis, Congressional action might occur only after serious damage has been done and costs have been significantly increased.

In considering privatizing Federal deposit insurance, therefore, the serious question becomes: How much less than the equivalent of a "full faith and credit" pledge by the Federal government will the public accept—in other words, how much less would fully protect the banking system in times of crisis? We do not know the answer, but history suggests that we cannot predict the depth or duration of a crisis, and that should make us wary.

The final question I want to ask today is: Would reducing the scope of deposit insurance bring positive results?

In this regard, one observer, former FDIC Chairman Bill Isaac, recently wrote in the *American Banker:* "What's needed is more private-sector discipline. This will come about once the scope of depositor protection is curtailed sharply, including abandonment of the 'too big to fail' doctrine. Millions of organizations and sophisticated individuals must be given the incentive to understand, monitor, and control the risks in the financial system."

I agree that market discipline is an important element of a sound deposit insurance system. Our goal is to assure the stability of the banking system in times of great stress, not to eliminate all bank failures. An effort to eliminate all bank failures would involve over-regulation of banks that would lessen their effectiveness in providing financial intermediation in the economy.

The question remains: What has been done to encourage market discipline and what more can be done? I will discuss these issues more in a moment, but first let's consider the issue of the scope of deposit insurance.

In terms of insuring individual deposits, the scope of coverage increased until 1980 and then declined, in terms of today's dollars. Let me explain.

As of January 1, 1934, the FDIC insured deposits up to $2,500. In 1996 dollars, however, that $2,500 is the equivalent of $30,000 today. Six months later, the insurance limit was raised to $5,000, which is almost $60,000 in today's dollars.

In 1969, the limit was raised to $20,000, which is about $85,000 in today's dollars. When the limit was raised to $40,000 in 1974, that was the equivalent of $127,000 today.

From its very beginning, deposit insurance covered more than just the average American's "food and rent" money—it was sufficient to cover some savings.

Moreover, depositors today are insured up to $100,000—a limit that has been in place since 1980. The dollars of 1980 are not the dollars of 1996, however—$100,000 in 1980 was the equivalent of $190,000 today. In this sense, for the individual depositor, the scope of deposit insurance coverage has declined by almost half since 1980.

I am not advocating any change in the level of today's coverage for deposits—the marketplace has already done that. Of course, the other side of the scope of insurance coverage is uninsured depositors and the so-called 'too big to fail' doctrine, as Bill Isaac points out. The Federal Deposit Insurance Corporation Improvement Act, however, significantly reduced the authority regulators have to deal with large institutions that are failing. It leaves us with enough flexibility, with appropriate oversight by Congress, to achieve a solution where the failure would present a genuine risk to the system. This can occur, however, only if the Secretary of the Treasury—in consultation with the President—determines that there would be "serious adverse effects on economic conditions or financial stability." Such a decision would be undertaken only after written favorable recommendations from both the FDIC Board of Directors and the Board of Governors of the Federal Reserve System, with at least two-thirds of the members of each body voting in favor of the recommendation. That is a high standard, particularly when one considers that the recommendation would have to be defended to the Congress.

Moreover, the FDIC has been required by law since 1991 to accept the proposal from a potential purchaser that is the least costly to the insurance fund of all the proposals we receive. In more than half of the failures in 1992—66 out of 120—uninsured depositors received less than 100 cents on each dollar above the $100,000. That was a significant increase in uninsured depositors experiencing losses from 1991, when fewer than 20 percent of the failures involved a loss for uninsured depositors. While the number of bank failures in 1992 was lower than in previous years, the number of uninsured depositors experiencing a loss was significantly greater. Moreover, as the paper that is the subject of the next panel points out, resolution with losses to uninsured depositors have not produced large-scale withdrawals at other institutions—though, in the years since 1992, with record levels of bank profits, failures slowing to a trickle, and no major bank threatened with failure, the system has not come under stress.

Further, I would ask, can depositors be expected to impose market discipline on banks? After all, it was this approach that led to the recurring banking panics that marked most of our history until 1933. A number of years ago, banking analyst Karen Shaw Petrou concisely described why the Congress created the FDIC to benefit individual Americans: "After the collapse of the early 1930s, it was agreed that individual savers should have a protected right to place a limited amount of money in a financial institution without having to worry that it could be lost. Individual depositors should not have to read a detailed report of a bank's condition before deciding where to deposit their retirement or other savings, since most depositors would be hard pressed to interpret such information. To solve the problem, the government took upon itself the obligation to interpret the financial condition of banks for depositors, and to back up its judgments with limited federal deposit insurance."

In standing in the place of the depositor, banking supervisors seek to mitigate the problem of moral hazard created by Federal deposit insurance through examinations and safety-and-soundness regulations.

The challenge to the regulators is to develop safety-and-soundness regulation that comes as close as possible to market discipline, without imposing inefficient, ineffective regulations on banks, regulations that unduly inhibit the important function of financial intermediation that they perform for the economy. Market discipline, however, does have a critical role in addressing the problem of moral hazard that deposit insurance creates—that discipline, however, can perhaps more effectively be imposed by large creditors and shareholders of banks.

At least since the least cost test has been imposed on the FDIC, large creditors should understand the potential for losses on their exposures to banks. That was perhaps less true with respect to earlier large-bank resolutions. In addition, over the past few years, we have undertaken two reforms in deposit insurance that give shareholders a greater incentive to curb excessive risk taking at their institutions: one is higher, risk-based, capital standards; the second is risk-related insurance premiums.

Higher risk-based capital standards expose shareholders of an institution to greater loss, and risk-based standards expose shareholders to greater loss as the institution's risks increase. Not incidentally, the regulations that put higher minimum capital standards into effect impose restrictions on dividend payments and other capital distributions if an institution falls below the minimum.

Similarly, risk-based premiums are designed to reduce income in institutions that take on excessive risk, and that reduction in income is aimed at giving shareholders reason to curb the excesses. As you know, in 1993, the FDIC established risk-based deposit insurance premiums. Banks and thrift institutions were divided into nine groups, depending upon the risks they present to their insurance fund.

Part of that risk calculation is based on capital and part on supervisory factors such as asset quality, loan underwriting standards, and management. We are now analyzing whether other factors are relevant to risk—and whether our current 27-basis point spread is sufficient to price the risks to the insurance fund posed by individual institutions. Making it more costly for banks to take on excessive risk will impose more economic discipline on their judgments.

In conclusion, in the 1980s and early 1990s, deposit insurance helped maintain financial stability, but at great cost, particularly with respect to the savings and loan industry.

We should learn from that experience.

Those lessons could lead us to continue to improve our current Federal deposit insurance system—as we have begun to do—to make it more sensitive and responsive to the marketplace—finding even better regulatory surrogates and incentives for marketplace discipline.

Some say that those lessons should lead us to replace the current system with a privatized approach. But before we take that course, we should agree on the answers to the questions: What would happen if there were no Federal deposit insurance program? Can a supplier other than the Federal government bear the costs necessary to provide deposit insurance coverage sufficient to maintain stability in the banking system in times of extreme stress? How much less than the equivalent of a "full faith and credit" pledge by the Federal government will the public accept?

Without firm answers to those questions, in privatizing Federal deposit insurance we may be putting the banking system at risk. We know Federal deposit insurance works to stabilize the banking system in times of great stress. Can we be sure that another approach will work as well?

Thank you.

Panel 3

Lessons of the 1980s:
What Does the
Evidence Show?

L. William Seidman
Robert E. Litan
Lawrence J. White
Stanley C. Silverberg

Panel 3

Lessons of the Eighties: What Does the Evidence Show?

The World Financial System: Lessons Learned and Challenges Ahead
L. William Seidman*

It is an honor to come to the land of the world's major banks to talk with you about international finance. At last count, four of the five largest banks in the world, and 15 of the largest 30 were based in your country. Japan and its international banking relationships are key players in a system where every major international bank can influence, or perhaps even threaten, the entire world of finance.

Coming from the United States, I suspect I am invited here primarily for two reasons. First, my country has experienced, and now recovered from, a banking and savings and loan and credit union problem of major proportions—clearly the worst difficulties since the Great Depression. About 2,000 institutions failed and two of the three deposit insurance funds had to be recapitalized. The S&L fund became a liability of the government at a cost of over $100 billion. Notably, the other two insurance funds were able to meet their obligations without cost to the taxpayer. These two funds were refinanced and recapitalized by the premiums of the institutions they served.

Second, I'm here because my government service covered this traumatic period of disaster and recovery. Thus, I can report from first-hand experience what happened to the U.S. financial system.

* The author is Publisher, *Bank Director Magazine* and Chief Commentator, CNBC-TV, and is the former Chairman of both the FDIC and the RTC. This address was delivered to NIKKIN, 7th Special Seminar on International Finance, in Tokyo on September 18, 1996.

I will use my experience to give you thoughts on a few of the major lessons we learned in the United States and also the lesson the U.S. learned in its relations to the world financial community. Given the extent of the problems, we in the U.S. are "long" on experience and if we don't learn a lot from these experiences, we will surely repeat our problems.

After reviewing lessons learned, my views on the major challenges ahead will conclude this statement. Obviously, this is an ambitious undertaking so please understand I will only highlight what seem to me to be the most important issues.

Lessons Learned

First, every major developed nation learned that it is possible to have serious banking problems despite a great variety of regulatory structures, deposit insurance systems and banking organizations. Nations like the United States with thousands of banks had problems. But so did countries with only a few major institutions such as Canada, England, Sweden, Norway and others. Nations with relatively small insurance funds like Japan and the United Kingdom had problems, as did the United States with a very large and comprehensive funding. It seems evident that government subsidies like deposit insurance cannot be determined to be the basic cause of the problem, though subsidies may affect its magnitude. Equally, countries with a large, hands-on regulatory system like the United States and those with much smaller ones like Japan and England had similar types and dimensions of system upset.

No developed country system escaped banking problems, though it must be noted that the rigid German regulatory system probably fared better than most. This rigid system, however, seems to create competitive problems of its own. No magic formula for supervision or financed system can be identified from the difficulties of the last decade.

In the United States, states have different types of regulatory structures. In Massachusetts, regulation was strict and in Texas, less rigid, but both states' banks had severe financial problems.

Thus, lesson one then must be that there is no "magic bullet" system that will ensure banking safety and soundness.

Second, when world-wide financial problems occurred, every country called upon the government to move in and deal with the situation. No country said let the market work without any government intervention. Moreover, with respect to large institutions, uniformly, the government adhered to what we label in the United States as the "too big to fail doctrine." All governments moved to protect the system from economic trauma that could result from large bank failures. The unwritten international banking code provides that governments will rescue large international banks from failure through guaranteeing their liabilities. Here in Japan, I believe you have recently given a blanket guarantee to stabilize the system.

When I was chairman of the FDIC, we held a world conference on "too big to fail." This meeting was something of a *failure* because a conference is in trouble when no one wants to talk about its major subject, the reason for the gathering taking place. But that was the situation at our conference in 1990. Uniformly, regulators hesitated to talk about rescuing failing institutions because even to speak about rescuing institutions might affect the way their management behaved. Thus, I labeled the "too big to fail" doctrine as an "unwritten code of international conduct." In the United States, we now have made government rescue more difficult to achieve but it is still available when necessary. The bank regulator is yet to be born that won't find a duty to "save the system" when the chips are down. Nor is a supervisor to be found that won't seek to increase supervision. As the result of its experience, the U.S. regulation system is more restrictive and regulatory than it was.

As Adam Smith recognized, banking is different. Thus, lesson number two must be that financial systems are not and probably never will be totally free market systems.

Third, the banking problems of the 80s and 90s came primarily, but not exclusively, from unsound real estate lending. It is instructive to note that the real estate boom and lending fiasco appears to have started in the United States. U.S. banks had been prevented from following their customers' desires to borrow with money-market instruments because of the U.S.'s Glass-Steagall prohibitions. This law allowed investment bankers to dominate the field. Our U.S. banks were losing the business of the larger borrowing companies.

As a result, in looking around for other kinds of loans to make, and seeking ways to maintain growth, the larger U.S. banks tried leveraged buyouts (LBOs) and Latin American loans. But the largest growth in lending was in new loans for commercial real estate. Previously, banks had done only short-term lending on commercial real estate construction. For example, by law, they could lend on a new office building solely for the construction period and were required to have a follow-on "take out" by a long-term lender, primarily insurance companies, as a part of the required package. When this requirement was repealed, many banks, large and small, began to make loans without "take outs" and real estate lending became the fastest-growing area in the banking business.

The change was sudden and dramatic. Prior to the 80s, U.S. banks' real estate loans were less than 10 percent of the portfolio. By the mid-80s, some banks had 50 to 60 percent of their loans in real estate. Real estate was "where the action was." Of course, this change and increase in availability in and of itself provided fuel for funding a new commercial building boom. "A builder will build if a financer will finance." Prices soared, construction skyrocketed and banks seemed prosperous. Inflation in the 70s had made real estate a very attractive option as it enhanced nominal value. The generous bank lending and inflationary pricing set off the real estate construction mania. Soon this same disease was affecting most of the developed world.

Excess real estate lending, powered by rapidly rising rents and prices, rapidly occurred worldwide. But more that anything else, real estate lending became the fashion, the "new" banking idea of the times.

Everywhere from Finland to Sweden to England to the United States to Japan to Australia, excessive real estate loans created the core of the banking problem. Some have maintained that government subsidies such as deposit insurance created a moral hazard, which caused institutions to behave in a non-market manner and therefore to take risks that they would not have taken without government subsidy. However, in looking around the world, the risks were taken without regard to whether the deposit insurance system was comprehensive as in the United States, minimal as in the UK, moderate as in Japan, or essentially non-existent as in New Zealand.

The critical catalyst causing the institutional disruption around the world can be almost uniformly described by three words: real estate loans. In the U.S., the problem was made even worse by allowing S&Ls to make commercial real estate loans in areas they knew little about. They were already in trouble because they borrowed "short" and lent "long" in financing the housing market.

Thus, our third lesson is that the biggest danger for financial institutions is lending based on excessive optimism generated about certain kinds of lending that are the fashion of the day.

Fourth, with bank failures and near failures occurring around the world, governments adopted different approaches to dealing with troubled financial institutions. In the situation where a few large institutions essentially were at the heart of the banking system, government used the approach that the United States had utilized in the Great Depression with the Reconstruction Finance Corporation (RFC). This approach required the government to take a direct financial position in the banks and to provide financial support until they could recover. Support might include buying out "bad assets" or providing investment to recapitalize the bank. Their continued existence was dependent on government support.

In contrast, in the United States during the 1980s, where thousands of institutions big and small were in trouble, a different approach was taken by the FDIC and the Resolution Trust Corporation (RTC).

The FDIC and the RTC "took over" failed institutions and protected their depositors, generally by selling deposits to another institution with accompanying funds to meet the obligations and then by disposing of their assets as rapidly as possible. In the United States, large institutions came to be handled through a new institution—a "bridge bank"—with the government creating a new bank and operating it as an owner until the institution could be disposed of privately. This system allowed the government to eliminate all liabilities and equity claims (except deposits) and start the bridge bank with a solvent balance sheet. Several insights can be gleaned from these experiences.

(a) First, each country's solution to its failing financial institutions requires a separate plan designed to meet the particular institutional structures of that country. And within the country, each institution may require different treatment based on individual situations. Size, condition, location, etc. will affect the method used.

(b) Second, in the U.S. every plan that succeeded sought to put the institutions back into the private sector with as little government support as could be used and still be effective. In the plans that did the best the government kept its involvement to the minimum activity required to return the institution to the private sector.

(c) Third, based on U.S. experience, the quicker the action taken to deal with insolvent institutions, the lower the cost and the faster the recovery of the financial system. The biggest mistake my administration made, in its early days, was to take over a failed institution, liquidate it, take out the assets and manage them till they could be sold. Later we learned it is much more efficient and quicker to maintain the failed institution, manage it, and sell the assets from there.

Bureaucratic attempts to delay action so that the problems will not become a political issue on their watch, as happened with the U.S. S&Ls, can only lead to increasing the cost of the solution.

(d) Fourth, where commercial real estate was involved, recovery requires re-establishing an active real estate marketplace so that troubled loans and nonperforming assets could be sold. This means selling to "venture buyers" at the start of the process. But as I often said, "The RTC never saw a buyer acting out of a sense of patriotic duty." Only with this action can the system become stabilized and the true condition of the institution be determined.

Thus, based on these insights, our fourth lesson can be that insolvent banks require government action, tailored to fit the individual situation, and the longer the corrective action is delayed the more costly and destabilized the problem will be. Of course, there were many other lessons to be noted; for example, the use of monetary policy to keep interest rates low and aid wounded banks to recover.

My final observation leads us to into the challenges of the years ahead. What encouraging things have we learned about our systems and its regulators when they were subjected to the great pressures of the last decade? We have seen remarkable resilience in the free market financial system of the developed countries in the world. In the face of the excesses of the real estate market and defaults on foreign debt, many systems were threatened but no system failed. The world system was jeopardized but it continued to function. Essentially, the marketplace did its job of self-correction, aided by large doses of government support at crucial times. In the U.S., every large bank that failed did so when the marketplace acted to force government assistance.

Thus, the fifth lesson can be that our faith in our international system, despite its flaws, actually was enhanced, perhaps to our surprise. Not only was the world financial system able to survive, but during this period international regulation was improved and the supervision of the system was changed in a fundamental way.

The Basle Committee of the IMF put into effect the first effective capital standards and procedures for the international banking community. These new rules were designed to ensure that undercapitalized banking by nations or individual banks did not jeopardize international banking. I have attended many world conferences during my government service. The Basle (Cooke) Committee's work and accomplishments stand out as the most successful effort in international cooperation I have ever seen. These lessons of the last decade hopefully can be used to help the banks and regulators as they meet the potential large challenges to the international financial system in the decade ahead.

Challenges Ahead

How can this wealth of experience be used to give us a transformation strategy for core competence in the financial system of the next decade? What are the key challenges ahead?

The *first challenge* is to deal with the problems left in the system by the last decade of excesses. The financial system is a bit like a chain—only as strong as its weakest link. The continuing problems in Japan are now well known and action appears to be underway to restore the health of the system. But clearly more decisive steps need to be taken to deal with the problem—and the sooner the better. The Japanese real estate market must be restarted by "biting the bullet" and taking the losses that sales will require. Other developed countries also have some clean-up work to do to restore their systems.

Little has been said about the banking problems of the newly developing countries or of those that were formerly part of the communist or socialist bloc market economies. Their financial system problems are just coming to light. The World Bank tells me of the 180 countries they cover, 130 are undergoing or recovering from a crisis in their banking systems. From Venezuela to India, from Lithuania to Kenya, and from Poland to China, banking systems suffer from bad loans made largely at the direction of controlling governments for political purposes or personal favoritism. A large international effort by all of the international agencies is underway to help bring those systems to an appropriate level of safety and soundness. This can only be done when the systems are fully privatized and needed legal infrastructures are put in place. This will not be easy, but correction of these problems from the past must be a part of the new core competence of the system of the future.

The second challenge is to move worldwide toward *full disclosure* in a free market. As the experience of the less-developed countries particularly underscores, the best banks operate with the deregulated *free market as the primary reg-*

ulator. Markets are self-correcting, though often late and drastic in their work. But to operate effectively, the marketplace needs *full disclosure and total transparency*. In the United States, the disclosure required by the SEC and bank regulators helped to keep most of the system's banks safe; and it helped regulators to close those that weren't. Much greater disclosure of all significant financial information worldwide is a real challenge to those who supervise the system. Only with full transparency can the free market work its wonders. Full disclosure, worldwide, will require some basic changes in philosophy in many countries. That is a real challenge, but it is essential for core competence in the years ahead.

The third challenge is to create effective international supervision of the world financial system. Supervisors, to work best, must concentrate on disclosure standards that are understandable and comparable around the globe. More is being done at the securities regulation level than at the banking level in this regard. Some sort of penalty must be developed for those countries and institutions that will not conform. Perhaps, restriction in use of the market system could be proposed. This was suggested for governments based on the recent exchange problems that came to light in Mexico. Such problems might have been less severe with more openness by the Mexican government.

In addition to supervision of disclosure, the regulators must and will continue to enhance capital standards and encompass new risks. In this regard, the evaluation of an institution's own system to measure risk is certainly the most effective supervisory method. This brings me to the next challenge.

The fourth challenge is for the banking system to operate successfully in the new technological environment. Banking was really the first business to be on an Internet-type system. Technology can create soundness or hinder it. Many have identified the globalization created by new technology as a threat to the world financial system. Its speed does create the potential for panic. Another danger is that technology also gives institutions the ability to create infinitely complex financial instruments. These new contracts are a two-edged sword, giving the banks and regulators the ability to hedge risk and also to misjudge it. The *challenge* is to *use* technology to develop systems that will aid safety and soundness, knowing all the while that it also has the potential to destroy.

I believe that technology has brought the possibility of doing a much better job of managing risk. Operating a financial institution has always been *about* managing risk, but technology with its modeling brings a powerful new tool of management. The new approach, which requires financial institutions to build their own models, holds great promise for a more effective and timely self-correcting system. Full disclosure of the risk profiles developed by institutions can provide the information for the core competence needed in a stable system.

Thus, new technology is essential in judging the risks of derivatives and other new financial instruments. New early-warning systems can also be developed. Any unusual activity in the world's market can be monitored. This is the way personal credit is monitored in the U.S. by some institutions. *Any unusual activity and the warning alarms begin to sound.*

Using new technology to aid market discipline, full disclosure, risk management and early-warning systems gives promise that a more core competent system can be developed in the future.

But there is a *final challenge* and that challenge is common to all areas of our wonderful new interrelated world. That challenge is the threat of organized or even isolated acts of terrorism. The terrorists of the world of finance are not bombers but are the rogue traders and rogue institutions, like BCCI, Sumitomo's copper trader and his lenders, Baring's Leeson and others who can operate to undermine the system, often with cover that escapes surveillance. Today's interrelationships are such that such rogues could seriously jeopardize an institution or even threaten the financial system in a country or parts of the world. Experience here tells us that most of the rogue traders were successful in their operations because their institutions or their regulators were inadequate in their policing of the individuals involved, or worse, were seduced by the profits the rogue produced to look the other way.

The ability of these defrauders to do great harm and bring down institutions has never been greater nor more difficult to control. Like the terrorists who kill, the subway gas bomber and the perpetrators of the Pan Am 107 bombing, financial terrorists are tough to catch and even harder to protect against. Yet in the modern internationally interdependent world system, they are ever more dangerous and destructive. And financial systems could be the target of the terrorists with bombs as well as false entries. Terrorism has no easy answer. That mundane word of accountants *"internal control"* will be the most important requirement of the day. Constant vigilance and the development of even more sophisticated systems will be the challenge to both the financial institutions and their regulators. The search for the most effective backup systems of internal control will be the never-ending duty of those in charge.

In conclusion, let me say there is little evidence that the future will change human nature and its weakness for over-enthusiasm and excessive pursuit of gain and a tendency of mankind to be *secretive*. Yet this aspect of human behavior lies beneath many of the challenges the financial system has faced in the last decade. I don't challenge those reasonable to change human nature. But perhaps it is fair to challenge the next generation to use technology, disclosure, supervision, cooperation and vigilance to successfully manage the "uncontrollable."

Comments on Lessons of the Eighties: What Does the Evidence Show?
Robert E. Litan*

I join the other commenters in applauding George on a thorough and well-researched paper. It will make a valuable addition to the literature. At the same time, I have several concerns about the paper and its analysis that I wish to highlight.

What Went Wrong in the 1980s?

George accurately describes the decade as one in which Murphy's law proved accurate—about everything that could have gone wrong did go wrong: banks lost their bread and butter business (commercial loans) to the commercial paper market, so they chased higher-risk LDC, real estate and LBO loans—many of which went sour; deep regional recessions in the Southwest in the early 80s and in New England at the end of the decade caused many otherwise healthy banks to topple; and many new banks entered the business and these failed at a higher rate than preexisting institutions. The paper strongly implies, if not explicitly states, however, that the one thing that went right during the 1980s was regulatory forbearance, initiated both by Congress and the regulators, which George argues gave many weak banks time to recover (although some banks took the opportunity offered by regulatory laxity to take deeper plunges).

While I agree with parts of this story line, I also have a couple of dissents or qualifications. First, it is important to note that the 1980s was not the first decade in which this country experienced deep regional recessions. I am old enough to remember the first oil shock of 1973–74, which sent many parts of the country that didn't produce oil—notably, states on the East Coast and in the Midwest—into a tailspin. Yet we had very few bank failures in the 1970s: Franklin National was one of the largest and its problems were due primarily to losses suffered in foreign exchange. Why, then, were there so many bank failures in the 1980s?

Part of the answer is that in the 1970s banks still hadn't lost much of their commercial lending franchise to the commercial paper market, as they did during the 1980s. But this is an incomplete answer because most of the bank failures in the 1980s—at least measured by the numbers—involved banks too small to have

---

* The author is Director, Economic Studies Program, The Brookings Institution.

been involved in much lending to companies who chose to issue commercial paper instead. More important, the loss of prime quality borrowers needn't have led banks to take *improperly priced* risks, as many of them did; after all, finance companies generally make riskier loans than banks do, but charge for it through higher lending rates, and so relatively few such companies have failed.

A good portion of the answer for why so many banks experienced troubles in the 1980s, therefore, must lie in the pernicious effects of moral hazard created by deposit insurance, compounded, of course, by the litany of factors that George cites in his paper. In fact, the 1980s proved to be the decade in which Congress and federal regulators collectively extended the safety net to virtually all banks in the system. While the insurance ceiling was formally raised in 1980 (from $40,000 to $100,000 per account), it was, as a practical matter, increased to much higher levels—indeed to uninsured deposits of any size—in the case of the many failed banks that were merged with healthier institutions, a process that de facto protected all depositors. Moreover, regulators *explicitly* protected uninsured depositors of several large banks that failed, including Continental Illinois, Bank of New England and the MCorp banks.[1]

It is not my purpose here today to question the wisdom of these actions; even with the luxury of 20–20 hindsight I can certainly sympathize with the desire of policymakers who had to wrestle with the Continental crisis to avoid a potentially damaging run on many major banks if the uninsured depositors of Continental had not been protected (the bank failed, after all, during a time of great anxiety about the health of money-center banks generally). But the blanket extension of protection to virtually all bank depositors during the 1980s had its price in undermining the incentives of managers of banks, especially large banks, to avoid taking excessive risks—a price which showed up in record deposit insurance losses during the decade and into the early 1990s.

Yet even with these perverse incentives, many bank failures could still have been avoided had full interstate banking (and branching) been in effect throughout the 1980s. It is well known, for example, that during the 1980s nine of the top ten banking organizations in Texas failed. It is not a coincidence that Texas also

---

[1] Indeed, in the case of Continental, policymakers even guaranteed uninsured creditors of the *holding company,* not just the bank.

severely restricted branch banking and for a time, prohibited out-of-state bank holding companies from coming into the state. While Texas suffered a deep recession during the decade, it is unlikely that all of the state's top banking organizations would have toppled had they been integrated into larger, nationwide institutions that would have spread their lending risks across different geographic regions. In this regard, it is unfortunate that apparently Texas has chosen to opt out of the nationwide branching law that is to become effective later this year.

Regulatory Forbearance

While George concedes that regulatory forbearance for thrifts in the 1980s proved to be a major mistake, he takes a more sanguine view of the practice for banks, which represents an implicit, if not explicit criticism of the "Prompt Corrective Action" (PCA) provisions of FDICIA (requiring regulators to take early actions as bank capital weakens, such as constraining bank growth unless they raise more capital, and taking over banks even before they are insolvent on a book value basis).

To be sure, George cites some data suggesting forbearance was costly: if PCA had been applied during the 1980s, then 340 banks that failed would have been closed or recapitalized earlier, saving an estimated 6 percent of their resolution cost, or about $600 million.[2] At the same time, however, George also seems to suggest that this cost was a small price to pay for the following "successes":

(1) that most of the banks classified as problem banks during the 1980–94 period did not fail, which suggests that allowing troubled banks breathing space—and not prematurely closing them or forcing their recapitalization or sale—was a good idea;

(2) that most banks granted forbearance because of their heavy concentrations of agricultural and energy loans that turned sour actually survived; and

(3) that losses of the banks that failed were not materially greater than the losses of other failed banks, suggesting that forbearance didn't make things worse.

---

[2] Readers should note that these figures were taken from a draft paper and so differ from those presented in Chapter 1 in volume 1 of this study (FDIC's note).

Furthermore, George argues that by focusing only on capital, as a way of avoiding forbearance in the future, FDICIA looks at a lagging indicator of weakness, suggesting that Congress has forced regulators to pay attention to the wrong measure.

These are interesting observations, but they overlook several other compelling considerations. First, and perhaps most important, the paper does not discuss what was probably the largest bank forbearance program of all during the 1980s—the fact that the regulators did not force the large banks that had big LDC debt exposures to mark their loans to market, and thus to replenish their depleted capital positions or to shrink. In fact, as already noted, regulators bailed out Continental's uninsured depositors in large part out of fear that otherwise depositors would run on other money-center banks that were then in trouble over LDC loans.

Defenders of "big bank forbearance" will no doubt argue that the policy "worked": other than Continental no money-center bank failed. But this version of history overlooks the fact that by not constraining the growth of weakened banks, regulators allowed them to gamble for recovery—in much the same way that many truly insolvent thrifts gambled for "resurrection"—by pouring tens of billions of dollars into commercial real estate and other high-risk loans on which the banks later had to take big writedowns. By looking only at the FDIC's losses from forbearance and neglecting the larger economy-wide resources that were wasted by banks that faced insufficient incentives to be prudent, the paper fails to properly measure the true total costs of forbearance.

Second, what I read to be an implicit criticism in the paper of the PCA requirements of FDICIA ignores the valuable *deterrent* effect of PCA, which has encouraged banks to push capital ratios above the regulatory minimum, as an insurance device, if you will, against suffering the costs or indignities of automatic regulatory intervention if at some point they are forced to weather unusually large losses again. This extra layer of capital that is now found in many banks has largely removed the danger of the country repeating the sorry episode of the 1980s, a valuable benefit of FDICIA.

Third, the paper argues that regulators were taking a tough line on weak banks in the 80s—even before FDICIA. This claim is inconsistent with some of the evidence Jim Barth, Dan Brumbaugh, and I looked at in 1990 when we studied the Bank Insurance Fund for the House Banking Committee. We found that in 1987 and 1989, two years when large banks took big hits on their loan portfolios, there were significant numbers of large banks (those having at least $1 billion in assets) that lost money yet nevertheless were allowed to pay dividends. This was true even for banks with capital ratios less than 6 percent, then considered to be a benchmark of health (39 in 1987 and 29 in 1989).

Fourth, while the paper is correct in arguing that capital, as measured by *book value,* is a lagging indicator of health, it should be pointed out that capital measured at *market value* almost by definition would provide a more current indication of a bank's true health. Yet it must also be recognized that for many of the nation's largest banks, with their increasingly sophisticated derivatives operations, even current market values may not provide a good signal of the bank's true risk exposure. This is because changes in the values of derivatives, as well as loan instruments themselves, can cause the market value of a bank's capital to move by significant margins from day to day, even by substantial amounts within the day. One of the challenges for regulators and market participants alike in the future is to harness the tremendous advances in information technology and communications to move in the direction of real time monitoring of banks, indeed of all financial institutions, so that these fluctuations in value can be more precisely determined and monitored.

In the meantime, I want to close with a suggestion for making the job of regulators easier—while also ensuring that they are not able again to be tempted to resort to forbearance strategies in the future, which I believe, on balance, are dangerous to pursue. The idea is not novel, but all the same, it's about time it should be implemented.

In brief, I believe that large banking organizations—say, those with assets of $10 billion or more—should be required to back some small portion of their assets (such as 1 percent) with long-term subordinated (and thus uninsured) debt. The debt should be staggered in maturity so that, even if a bank didn't grow, it would have to regularly (quarterly) go to the market to sell its debt. And just to be clear, I would impose the requirement on *banks,* and not their holding companies (which do not rely on insured deposits).

Why subordinated debt? One important reason is that it is a stable source of funds: unlike holders of uninsured deposits who can run on a moment's notice, holders of subordinated debt are stuck with their investments until maturity (or until they can persuade someone else to take the securities off their hands). As a result, investors in uninsured subordinated debt have very strong incentives to encourage banks to avoid imprudent risks, as well as to disclose a maximum amount of information (yes, even balance sheets marked-to-market) that would be useful to investors.

Subordinated debt is also better than capital at disciplining a bank because holders of the debt do not share in the upside of a bank's gains, and thus have no incentives to encourage gambling. At the same time, the amount of subordinated debt cannot be manipulated, unlike equity, which consists in part of retained earnings (which can be manipulated through various devices—lenient loss reserving being just one example).

Finally, subordinated debt also disciplines regulators. Weak banks that cannot sell their debt in the market at reasonable terms will not be able to grow and take more risks. As a result, regulators cannot engage in forbearance even if they want to. And that is one lesson from the 1980s that should not be forgotten.

The Lessons of the 1980s for Bank Regulation: An Overview of the Overview
Lawrence J. White[*]

The 1980s and early 1990s were an extraordinary era for depository institutions and for their regulators. Failures of commercial banks and of savings institutions occurred in numbers that had not been seen since the early 1930s—indeed, in numbers that the regulatory reforms of the 1930s were supposed to have precluded.

The Federal Deposit Insurance Corporation (FDIC) should be warmly commended for its decision to commission a set of studies ("History of the Eighties—Lessons for the Future") that is intended to assess this experience for commercial banks (and their regulators) and to distill the lessons for future regulation. Having read three of the papers, I am eager to see the remainder of the papers from this Project; I believe that they will add significantly to our understanding of that turbulent period.

In these comments I will first briefly discuss George Hanc's overview paper, "A Summary of the Project Findings." I will then expand on a number of themes that arose at the January 16, 1997, Symposium at which three of the Project's papers ("A Summary of the Project Findings," "Bank Examination and Enforcement, 1980–1994," and "Off-Site Surveillance Systems in the 1980s and Early 1990s") were presented.

A. Hanc's Paper

George Hanc's "Summary. . ." is a clear statement of the findings of the other papers and of many of the problems that arose in commercial banking in the 1980s. It is well written and will improve most readers' understanding of what went wrong during that decade.

But, alas, at the end Hanc is too restrained. We don't learn what Hanc, with the benefit of "20–20 hindsight," would recommend that the FDIC should have done differently. And, given that hindsight, what are the "Lessons for the Future" that should be learned?

Though the Symposium was not about the S&L debacle of roughly the same

* The author is the Arthur E. Imperatore Professor of Economics at the Stern School of Business, New York University. From November 1986 until August 1989 he was a Board Member of the Federal Home Loan Bank Board.

period, I know what the benefit of 20–20 hindsight would cause me to recommend that my predecessors at the Federal Home Loan Bank Board should have done differently (or should have recommended strongly that the Congress do differently):

- S&Ls should have been deregulated in 1960 and 1962, not 1980 and 1982, in terms of their ability to have wider asset powers and to originate adjustable-rate mortgages (ARMs).

- Regulation Q (which placed ceilings on the interest rates that could be paid on deposits) ought not to have been extended to S&Ls in 1966 or should have been repealed in 1970, not 1980.

- The headquarters of the Ninth District of the Federal Home Loan Bank System should have been moved from Little Rock to Dallas in 1973, not 1983.

Even if none of these actions had occurred, my 20–20 hindsight would cause me still to recommend that the deregulatory actions of the 1980–1982 period should have proceeded; but they should have been accompanied by:

- More examiners and supervisors, not fewer.

- Tougher capital standards, not weaker.

- A better accounting system (market value accounting), not one that allowed goodwill assets to be freely created when there were no underlying values.

- An assignment of examiners and supervisors from other districts to the Dallas (Ninth District) office in 1983–1985, to help cover the personnel shortages that arose in that office after the move from Little Rock.

- Tighter limits on annual growth by any individual S&L.

- A strong memo to all FHLBB personnel that George Bailey (as portrayed by Jimmy Stewart in "It's a Wonderful Life") was no longer the CEO of any S&L in their jurisdiction.

Though these are the specific actions that should have been applied to the actual historical experience, they carry clear implications for future policy.[1] I hope that Hanc—either as part of this Project or in another forum—will distill clearly from the studies the "should have been done" and "therefore should be done" implications for commercial banks and their regulation.

Let me now turn to some recurrent themes of the Symposium.

---

[1] I have previously outlined my beliefs about the implications for regulation. See Lawrence J. White, *The S&L Debacle: Public Policy Lessons for Bank and Thrift Regulation*. New York: Oxford University Press (1991).

B. Rules versus Discretion

It is the natural inclination of regulators to want discretion. I know that this is so; I've been there. Rigid rules never have enough flexibility to allow the "right" outcomes under all circumstances. Hence, we need discretion.

But discretion can be abused. In the early 1980s discretion toward S&Ls became "forbearance," and the eventual costs were quite high.

In reality, the choice is never between "only discretion" and "no discretion;" instead, we are always on a slippery slope somewhere in between, with the necessity of making tradeoffs. But in the process of considering those tradeoffs, we need to shed at least one important piece of mythology that still mistakenly guides too much policy in the bank regulation area.

That mythology is exemplified by the giant-sized photographs that adorn the walls of the auditorium where the Symposium was held. They show worried men and women in lines outside failed or failing banks, hoping that their deposits have not evaporated. These are marvelous photographs and an important reminder of why deposit insurance is a vital part of today's banking world.

But a second look at the photographs shows that they are all vintage shots of the 1930s. There are good reasons why this is so. Equivalent photos could not have been taken during the past 60 years.[2] This phenomenon doesn't happen any more. Even when the FDIC has to close an insolvent bank, the agency almost always does so after the close of business on a Friday, and the bank typically re-opens with new owners (and often a new name) on Monday. But virtually all depositors are unaffected. Even in the rare instance when the FDIC actually closes a bank permanently and liquidates the assets, the insured deposits are moved to a neighboring bank, or the checks are ready for the insured depositors by that Monday.

Nevertheless, the mythology of shuttered banks and forlorn depositors queuing in the street to get the bad news about their deposits still dominates too much of regulatory policy.

Specifically, consider bank closures and the tradeoffs between mistakenly delaying closure (excessive discretion) and mistakenly closing a bank prema-

---

[2] Perhaps there were somewhat similar photos that were taken in the mid-1980s when state-chartered thrifts in Maryland and Ohio failed and their state-sponsored deposit insurance funds also failed; but such photos would not be available in the cases of failures of federally insured institutions.

turely (insufficient discretion).[3] The costs of inadequate monitoring and delayed closure can be quite high, as the S&L debacle illustrated. The costs of premature closure also are not trivial. As Stephen Steinbrink reminded the Symposium, closure removes the owners and (usually) the top managers and affects their reputations; the FDIC should not do this casually or without sufficient cause. But the notion that bank closures are catastrophic events for communities (as illustrated by the photographs on the wall), and therefore should be avoided at almost any cost, is simply a relic from another era that (thankfully) the FDIC has buried in practice and that (hopefully) the agency soon will put to rest in thought as well.

In sum, the tradeoffs between discretion and strict rules, and thus between delayed and early closures, should be considered on the basis of the real costs and benefits of each route and not by the outdated mythology of bank closures as catastrophic community events.

C. The Dangers of Narrow "Back-Casting" or Extrapolation

As an illustration of the potential costs of rigid rules, the Project conducted a statistical exercise to "back-cast" the application of the "prompt corrective action" (PCA) rules imposed by the Federal Deposit Insurance Corporation Improvement Act (FDICIA) of 1991 to the experience of the 1980s. The studies found that the imposition of the rules would have caused the "unnecessary" closure of 143 thinly capitalized banks. (Their closure would have been "unnecessary" in the sense that these 143 banks actually survived and did not require eventual closure). But, as Hanc points out in a footnote, the actual numbers of banks that would have been so closed would have been different from 143, because the presence of PCA would have changed some (or, perhaps, many) bank owners' and managers' behaviors; specifically, they likely would have avoided some activities and/or raised capital earlier if they had believed that the PCA rules would apply to them, so the number of prematurely closed institutions would have been less. Steinbrink made the same point in his oral remarks at the symposium.

This point is too important to be relegated to a footnote. To be sure, the complete modeling of the likely behavior of banks in the 1980s with the counterfactual presence of PCA is an extremely complex task; I do not wish to belittle the necessary effort nor claim that I could easily do it myself. And, yes, the simple

---

[3] Another dimension of regulatory policy that is driven by the "shuttered-banks-and-queuing-depositors" mythology is the insistence that banks' examination reports be kept confidential and not released to the public—presumably, so as to avoid depositors' runs on banks in response to unfavorable examination reports.

back-casting does give us a useful benchmark. But that benchmark should be seen as just the upper bound, with the likely number of prematurely closed banks being smaller, probably considerably so (and the consequences of the premature closure would not be catastrophic, for the reasons discussed above).

The same point applies to the prospective application of market value accounting (MVA) to banks. Opponents of its application frequently cite the volatility of banks' earnings that would thereby be revealed—an implicit statement about the results of back-casting MVA onto historical bank financial results. But the actual consequences of the imposition of MVA would surely be that banks would change their investment behavior (including the acquisition of hedges, the shortening of maturities of debt securities held, and other smoothing devices) so as to reduce the volatility reported under MVA.[4] Such changes would not be costless. But the debate ought to be focused on the benefit-cost tradeoffs of the induced reduction in that volatility[5] and not on the past levels of volatility that generally accepted accounting principles (GAAP) have masked and that MVA would have revealed.

D. Where Was the Risk?

Reidhill and O'Keefe's paper presents a careful analysis of all of the potential elements that might have led to banks' downfalls. Their conclusion, which is also found in Hanc's paper, is that high loans/assets ratios were the best leading indicator of a bank's likelihood of subsequently failing.

Though I do not question the substance of Reidhill and O'Keefe's methods, I wonder if high loans/assets ratios themselves really were the culprit[6]—or whether these high ratios were really indicators of some underlying elements of riskiness that the data are not capturing.[7] After all, modern finance theory has come to understand that an important comparative advantage of banks is as infor-

---

[4] Similarly, if bank owners and mangers know that examination reports will be made public and that such revelation might sometimes be embarrassing, they are likely to change their behaviors so that the underlying conditions that give rise to embarrassment are less likely to occur.

[5] As is clear from the discussion below, I believe that the benefits would exceed the costs.

[6] Also, the identification of high loans/assets ratios as the risky element has the flavor of the 1960s, when loans were considered risky and debt securities were considered safe for a bank.

[7] Reidhill and O'Keefe also find that rapid growth rates in assets and in loans are significantly associated with subsequent failure rates. This finding has considerably more appeal, since rapid growth is likely to place stress on any organization—leading to errors and possibly losses. Reidhill and O'Keefe do not present any correlation coefficients between loans/assets ratios and growth rates; if they are positive and high (as I would guess they are), the high loans/assets ratios may well be a proxy for rapid growth and other risky strategies.

mation processors and monitors of loans that are made to firms and individuals who are too small and/or too informationally opaque to be able to access securities markets. Equivalently, banks' comparative advantage is generally not in investing in publicly traded debt securities but rather in making loans.

Consequently, I urge extreme caution in interpreting these results as indicating that high loans/assets ratios for banks are automatically a suspicious characteristic worthy of regulatory scrutiny. And in any event, as the papers suggest (and, indeed, they ought to emphasize), any reliance on static ratio tests for discerning risk must be supplemented by forward-looking stress tests.

E. The Quality of the Information

The accounting system used by banks is the crucial determinant of the quarterly Call Report data, the determination of a bank's profitability, the calculation of the bank's capital, and ultimately (as Steinbrink reminded the Symposium) the basis for the regulators' being able to take legal actions vis-à-vis an errant bank. Reported insolvency is always a comforting piece of evidentiary support for nervous agency lawyers when a receivership for a bank is being contemplated.

But, unlike a system of weights and measures, the GAAP accounting system that is the standard today has no physical reality; a bank's capital (or net worth) cannot be measured in the same physical way that tons of grain or barrels of oil can be measured. Instead, GAAP provides a set of definitions and rules that guide the arithmetic of balance-sheet and profit-and-loss statement calculations. The GAAP definitions and rules are generally oriented toward backward-looking, cost-based valuations—which are more appropriate for a "stewardship" notion of accounting than for using the accounting information as an indicator of whether a bank may be sliding toward (or may have already reached) true (market value) insolvency that will be costly to the deposit insurance fund (and possibly to uninsured depositors).

In this context, then, it is clear that GAAP has not served bank regulators well. This inadequacy of GAAP arose a number of times in the papers and in the discussions at the Symposium, explicitly and implicitly:

- In the "Examination and Enforcement" paper, the FDIC found that regulatory supervisors were reluctant or unable to bring sufficient pressure on the managements of banks that the supervisors knew were sliding downward, so long as their GAAP accounts continued to show profitability. It was stated that bank capital can be a "lagging" indicator.

- Joe Peek's oral comments reminded the audience that, when a bank is starting to experience financial problems, it often sells its strongest assets—those with market values above their book values, so as to recognize the gains—while retaining its "underwater" assets (with market values below book values) on its balance sheet at book value. With systematic behavior of this kind, the bank's balance sheet would soon represent a significant overstatement of the value of the bank's assets and thus an overstatement of the bank's capital.

- Steinbrink lamented that too often the closure of a bank was delayed beyond when it should have happened, because of the delays in GAAP accounting to register asset losses.

- Reidhill and O'Keefe's findings indicated that the Call Report data of a bank's condition (essentially, GAAP accounting data) were not very useful in predicting bank failure five years into the future (but did provide useful predictions three years in advance); and high return-on-assets (ROA) ratios in 1984 and after were associated with bank failures after 1984 (again indicating a serious drawback to relying on GAAP).

- Finally, Mark Flannery reminded the Symposium that if the regulators insist on expressing their rules in terms of GAAP book value, they "deserve everything [too many costly bank failures] that they get."

There is a cure for these problems: moving to a current-looking market value accounting (MVA) system. If MVA were combined with on-site examinations (so that examiners can assess directly the quality of management) and forward-looking stress tests, bank regulators then would truly have the proper tools to do their jobs.

There is a conundrum here, however. My call for MVA is not new; I and others have been making this plea for over a decade. Despite slow movement in this direction by the Financial Accounting Standards Board (FASB), the basic backward-looking structure of GAAP (and the accompanying mindset of bank executives and their accountants) has remained largely unchanged. Indeed, bank regulators have resisted efforts to strengthen their own hands in this respect.

Why? The banking industry has resisted[8] for obvious reasons, since GAAP accounting gives them a free option that they can use to gain time for themselves:

---

[8] Also, the industry's accountants have resisted—perhaps because MVA would require them to "tool up" for a different system, and perhaps because it would require them to become value estimators, a role that they are probably reluctant to adopt.

sell "above-water" assets to show gains, while keeping "underwater" assets on their balance sheets at book value and hoping that the latter's market value will rise again. But why have the regulators resisted? Perhaps they all have been "captured" by the industry on this point; I don't think so, but it's a possibility. Alternatively, harking back to my earlier point concerning rules versus discretion, I think that an MVA system gives regulators less discretion (in the sense that they will have less room to forbear from forcing writedowns when their judgment is that the bank can be turned around). Or perhaps the sheer newness of an MVA system and the difficult questions that would arise in the transition from the "known" existing GAAP to a new MVA system are too daunting.

In any event, I find it to be a political-economy puzzle that regulators have been so opposed to considering MVA.[9]

F. Conclusion

There is much to be learned from the experience of the 1980s. The FDIC has made a good start in compiling and analyzing the data from that era. I look forward to reading more of the reports of the Project as they become available.

---

[9] Indeed, today—and probably the next few years—would be an ideal time for the adoption of MVA: The overwhelming majority of banks are profitable and would not be seriously (adversely) affected by MVA. They wouldn't like it (for the reasons mentioned in the text), but they could live with it today. That same statement could not have been made six or seven years ago; the industry would have fought MVA with all of its political might (because of how adversely it would have affected many of the industry's members). In this political-economy sense, then, the stars are aligned favorably; but I fear that no one will find it worthwhile to take any initiative in this respect.

Lessons of the 1980s: Some Comments
Stanley C. Silverberg*

George Hanc has written a very comprehensive and well-balanced paper on the 1980s, and I find little to disagree within the principal thrust of his paper. In the brief time I have been given, I would like to make a few selective points on (1) the causes of the bank problems and failures in the 1980s; (2) the impact of early resolution and forbearance; (3) the role played by deposit insurance; and (4) the future role for deposit insurance and bank supervision.

1. Why Did So Many Banks Fail in the 1980s?

George Hanc is correct in emphasizing the wide swings in economic activity, in commodity prices, in prices generally, and in interest rates. Another important consideration was the fact that we had gone so many years with so few commercial bank failures—the bankers who had been around during the 1930s had all died or retired. Of the various "causes" cited, I would be inclined to place greater stress on commercial real estate than George Hanc and other speakers have done. There were several special factors in the commercial real estate market:

- Savings and loans (S&Ls) were given expanded lending authority in 1982 federal legislation and through state legislation in California, Texas and elsewhere. Many S&Ls combined incompetence with a desperate need to increase income.

- The 1986 tax legislation made investment in commercial real estate less attractive and made it much harder to sell troubled real estate.

- Bank regulators had little experience in evaluating commercial real estate loans, and prevailing accounting practices that permitted capitalizing interest for several years on such loans did not provide the appropriate flags to alert bank supervisors of existing problems. Some have suggested that earlier recognition and action by bank examiners would not have mattered. Perhaps not.

- There was also the fact that somebody else's bad loan (whether or not an S&L made it) could adversely affect the performance of what otherwise would have been a good bank loan. The impact of others' mistakes was significant, whether that was S&Ls in Texas, savings banks in Massachusetts or Japanese commercial banks in California.

---

* The author is an independent consultant; from 1979 to 1987 he served as Director for Research and Strategic Planning at the FDIC.

Commercial real estate problems in the 1980s contributed to bank problems and failures, and, I believe, poor credit judgment by banks and thrifts exacerbated the commercial real estate problem and its impact on the overall economy. Hindsight also suggests that some of the strong economic performance in the second Reagan term came at the expense of the economic performance during the Bush presidency.

High nominal and real interest rates during much of the 1980s also contributed to bank failures. During the late 1980s when nonperforming loans rose dramatically, very high carrying costs placed a heavy burden on weak banks. While there was much discussion a few years back about how the Fed saved the banking system by reducing interest rates, a careful review of rates in the late 80s and early 90s suggests that the Fed was very slow to ease monetary policy during that period—for example, the federal funds rate averaged over 8 percent in 1990 even though real GDP was declining.

2. Forbearance and Early Resolution

We are all familiar with the many reasons why forbearance is bad: operating losses continue; if the bank is going to fail, then the franchise value is likely to shrink; bank management focuses on what can boost short-term performance, allowing longer-term values to deteriorate; there are apt to be fire sales on those pieces of the bank that have value; and, worst of all, management has an incentive to roll the dice on risky activity. Like so many *obvious truths,* we can point out situations where forbearance allowed banks that were probably insolvent to survive or to merge without any Government assistance. And we can cite a few cases where relatively large banks would have survived or merged if the regulators had moved more slowly (Southeast, First City, and PSFS). George Hanc points out that the farm bank program and, to some degree, the mutual savings bank net worth assistance program allowed a lot of institutions to survive and probably saved money for the FDIC. These programs generally included oversight and restraint on risk taking that served to restrain the potential cost of forbearance.

The worst forbearance in the 1980s occurred among the S&Ls where capital standards and accounting rules were relaxed, where growth by marginally solvent or insolvent S&Ls was encouraged, and where weak institutions were permitted to or encouraged to acquire still weaker institutions. In these situations, continued operation and rapid growth generally led to increased insolvency.[1] In addition, banks and stronger S&Ls were exposed to aggressive competition for deposits, loans, and services from undercapitalized institutions[2] and may have suffered the effects of bad commercial real estate lending as discussed above. Rigorous enforcement of capital requirements is a clear remedy for this problem.

The concept of *early resolution* was not invented in FDICIA. In principle, I believe, it had been part of the supervisory armory for many years. However, enforcement was uneven, and regulators were sometimes overly concerned about potential legal challenges to *early* closings. When a bank got into difficulty, it was pressed to write off bad loans and recapitalize ("stop being insolvent"). If it wasn't able to raise capital it would look for a buyer, and many failures were forestalled through such transactions, whether or not bank regulators played an active role. However, there were many situations where bank management underestimated its problems or overestimated the bank's value. Deposit insurance, slow action by regulators and limited disclosure helped keep stock prices of troubled banks at unrealistically high values. As a result, bank-saving private-sector mergers sometimes did not come off even though the raw material was there for such mergers. The failure of Franklin National in 1974 was a notable example of this.

While early resolution may save some money for the FDIC in bank failures that cannot be forestalled, I believe the principal case for an early resolution policy is that it affords a more credible threat for bank regulators, and pushes troubled banks to seek solutions while they still have value: while they still can raise capital or merge without Government assistance. In some cases the awareness of early resolution practice may be sufficient to get banks to act without pressure from the regulators. Early resolution also removes some discretion from bank regulators,[3] and while that's probably good, we should not get carried away about the value of hard and fast rules. In any case, departures from the practice will presumably require some conscious, thought-out policy.

FDICIA was enacted in December 1991, and became effective a few months later. Bank stock prices began to move up from very depressed levels in early

---

[1] The FDIC's track record here was less than perfect (e.g., Seamen's Bank for Savings, FSB where the FDIC shared supervision with the Federal Home Loan Bank System).

[2] This used to be referred to as the "airline problem."

[3] It is my impression that the FDIC has, in fact, tolerated some exception from early resolution, and I can think of one New York savings bank where that has apparently worked.

1991 for reasons wholly unrelated to FDICIA. The common thread was that the bank failure problem had passed its peak. The stock market apparently recognized this. Congress (and the FDIC) did not. Early resolution works very well when the market places reasonable or high valuations on bank franchises. However, in, say, 1990, the stock prices of several of the most conservatively run banks were well below book value. Investors and other banks were reluctant to pay positive prices for troubled banks without FDIC assistance. That has changed considerably during the past several years. Stock prices of thrifts came back somewhat later, and that too has led to unassisted acquisitions of troubled institutions.

An interesting question is: did the exaggeration of bank problems by many pundits, academicians, OMB, the FDIC, etc. have any impact on the market for bank stocks, and, if so, did this affect bank failures in 1990–91?

3. Deposit Insurance Coverage

For a while it was fashionable to blame deposit insurance for the bank failure problem of the 1980s, and apparently there are many today who blame deposit insurance for restrictions on bank activities[4] and intrusions on bank practices in many areas. I believe that the high level of insurance coverage was a very important factor in contributing to the S&L failures—when combined with the absence of meaningful capital requirements, forbearance, etc. However, I believe that deposit insurance and the very high level of nominal and *de facto* coverage were only marginal contributors to bank failures.

In his paper George discusses the Continental transaction. Continental was never a realistic candidate for a payoff. Not because of correspondent banks whose resulting problems could have been addressed with receivership certificates. The three federal bank regulators were all concerned, rightly or not, with the impact of the Continental payoff for Manufacturers Hanover and other large troubled commercial banks. And there was also the fact that the FDIC did not have the system and capability to pay off Continental's depositors in a reasonable time period and without looking incompetent.

A better payoff prospect was the First National Bank of Midland, Texas, which was closed in October 1983, several months after it was apparent that the

---

[4] Deposit insurance exists in Canada and the EU countries, and that has not gotten in the way of allowing banks to perform most financial services through subsidiaries or directly within the bank.

bank was insolvent. When it was closed it had assets of about $1.4 billion and deposits of only $575 million. Federal Reserve advances replaced large deposits and that made a cost test finding for a P&A possible. The bank had a modest number of deposit accounts (about 60,000), and, a few months earlier, a large percentage of uninsured deposits. The ultimate loss on the bank was $400–500 million. This was a potential payoff that the FDIC could have handled. It is interesting to speculate whether paying off Midland a year or so after the Penn Square payoff would have slowed bank loan growth in Texas and elsewhere and moderated some of the banking problems during the next several years.

It is very difficult to simulate a U.S. banking system in the 1980s with much lower *de facto* insurance coverage—presumably banks would have been more vulnerable to deposit flights and this would have affected their portfolio policies. Would the Fed have necessarily been a more willing lender? Would the cost of lower coverage have been much higher interest margins to compensate for reduced leverage or reduced risk in general? FDIC practice has generally been to focus on the immediate transaction and its impact on the next transaction rather than the longer-term considerations. On the other hand, however, many of the critics of FDIC practices have not always examined the immediate or longer-run implications of their proposed alternatives.

Overall, I think the deposit insurance system performed reasonably well in handling bank failures. George Hanc provides data on the number of bank failures and deposit insurance losses. Between 1982 and 1992, cumulative failures among FDIC-insured banks amounted to about 10 percent of banks with about 10 percent of domestic deposits. Cumulative insurance losses amounted to about 1.5 percent of average outstanding domestic deposits, so that these *unusually* large losses could have been covered by an average deposit insurance assessment rate of less than 0.15 percent of deposits—a cost that could be easily borne by the banking system, and, in fact, was.

FDICIA has made it harder to avoid imposing losses on larger depositors in bank failures, and it has made it more difficult for the Fed to fund deposit outflows in insolvent banks—my preference would have been not to allow the Fed to take collateral on its advances. It might be desirable if the level of deposit insurance coverage were reduced—but that's not going to happen. It wasn't even possible to reduce coverage modestly by simplifying the various separate capacities associated with insurance coverage. And what member of Congress would vote to reduce the $100,000 figure when everything is going well just because a bunch of economists are concerned about something called *moral hazard*? As for eliminating the Government guarantee, I doubt that it would be possible to convince anyone that the guarantee won't be there, if needed. I have no problem with privatizing the FDIC if it is possible to separate insurance from supervision. However, I believe that the case for reducing various forms of Government intrusion can stand on its own, and, in any case, has little to do with deposit insurance.

4. Future Role for Deposit Insurance and Bank Regulation

During the past several years most everything has gone well for banks and thrifts. There have been few failures, and earnings have achieved record levels, not only in absolute terms, but measured as a percentage of assets and capital. Bank performance has benefited from the combination of a growing economy, relatively stable prices and relatively stable interest rates. Apart from economic factors, which are extremely important, institutional factors are also contributing to an environment where there are likely to be fewer failures. These factors include:

- The experience of the 1980s probably has made bankers more cautious about lending, concentrations and internal controls.

- Disclosure has improved. Bank analysts and large customers use output from bank reports, and the quality of data in those reports has improved for several reasons, including more cautious behavior by accounting firms.

- Capital requirements are now uniformly monitored and enforced so that banks are pushed to rectify shortfalls early. In addition, banks no longer have to compete with banks and thrifts whose pricing reflects excessive leverage.

- Early intervention is also likely to force troubled banks to look for help while they still have positive value. High valuations of bank stock have made it much easier to find help.

- The failures and/or absorptions of so many banks and thrifts have lessened some excessive competition, although geographic expansion through branching and computer-based services may more than offset this reduction in competition.

- Most banks have had an opportunity to eliminate or write off longer-term, low interest-rate loans and investments.

- Banks appear to have become more "bottom line" oriented. Why? Capital requirements; experience with high deposit insurance premiums?

Despite the factors cited above, it is hard to explain why banks are performing so well, and not just compared with the 1980s.

In this improved environment, what should be the role of bank supervision? I believe that supervision should focus on overall policies of banks, particularly on their controls in key areas. In addition, it is important to verify that bank reports are accurate. That does not mean looking at all loans or even a high percentage of loans for good banks whose reporting is accurate, based on sampling. I suspect that better coordination of on-site and off-site supervision can provide good results in a less intrusive manner. Annual examination requirements should be handled flexibly. I also believe there are opportunities for greater coordination between bank supervision and audits by accounting firms, and it may be helpful to study practices in Canada and elsewhere.

Panel 4

The 1980s
in Retrospect

Paul A. Volcker
Carter H. Golembe
William M. Isaac
John G. Medlin, Jr.
Discussion

The 1980s in Retrospect

Paul A. Volcker*

I am glad that Chairman Helfer invited me to this affair because it got my juices going about banking supervision and regulation—a subject close to my heart. I read those papers and I thought they were clearly written and very helpful. I used to think I knew something about this subject, but I have to say that I have lost confidence in myself in the face of rapidity of change. It is partly the change in the banking system and partly my growing age and declining analytic skill. But, in any event, I am glad to have this excuse to get back in the middle of thinking about it

Now, in the interest of full disclosure, I have to tell you I'm a bank director these days. It has not been my life-long ambition, but somehow I have ended up there. I do have to report that it gives one a somewhat different perspective on some of these questions—even though I am relatively new. I was struck in the first few meetings that I went to at Bankers Trust how much of the agenda was directed by the Federal Reserve. I am sure most people feel that is a bureaucratic intrusion. I sat there thinking how sensible most of these requirements were. I realized I wrote a number of them.

In any event, the job of the moderator is to pose some issues. I want to pose a few and get on to the people who are going to discuss them. A lot of what I might have said is really redundant after that splendid speech by Chairman Helfer. She focused on some key issues. But, I do have one complaint about our particular listing on the program. It says this panel—and I am conscious that we are at the end of the program—is concerned with the 1980s in retrospect. The whole conference title, "Lessons for the Future," may be more appropriate. I think we really ought

---

* Paul A. Volcker was Chairman of the Board of Governors of the Federal Reserve System from August 1979 to August 1987, and before that spent more than four years as President of the Federal Reserve Bank of New York.

to be focusing less on the 1980s in retrospect and more on the lessons for the future.

What strikes me in reading this material for the 1980s is how much has changed in the 1990s and is in the process of change. I have no doubt that if we had these papers somehow available at the beginning of the 1980s—that by some great process we could have absorbed the lessons of the 1980s before the 1980s took place—we would not have had many of the problems of the 1980s. But I'm not sure I could say the same thing about the 1990s because so much has changed. Would these same lessons be adequate for, say, 2007?

I do think we will continue to have these difficult questions of balancing official protection against market discipline. Let me just say quickly that I think the attitudes in that respect do change greatly depending upon where you sit. The 1980s exposed various excesses which I think, to some degree, were becoming apparent in the 1970s. I can remember very clearly sitting in my office then, as President of the Federal Reserve Bank of New York, thinking what this country needs is a first-class bank failure to teach us all a lesson—but please God, not in my District. When I went to Washington, I had the same feeling—we need a clear lesson from market discipline, but please dear God, not in my country. Then, if I read correctly the 1990s, and what happened when the Mexican crisis came along, Bob Rubin and Alan Greenspan thought what we need is a good country failure to teach everybody a lesson, but please not a large country in my hemisphere. I really want to emphasize a point that Bill Seidman made earlier—whatever the talk about the technicalities of deposit insurance, the particular level of it and whether or not you have it, and how much you theoretically want to rely upon market discipline, there isn't a developed country in the world in the 1980s and early 1990s that did not run into banking crisis. I don't know of any of those countries that didn't act to protect the banking system with assistance whatever the law said. The creditors and depositors didn't get hurt if it was a bank of any size. That included good, conservative, market-oriented Scandinavian banks, where the banking systems were almost wholly taken over for a time by the government.

Market discipline can be very important. We like to use it. But I remind those who want to rely upon it wholly of some simple facts. I can't remember any banks that failed who didn't have a clean auditing statement, sometimes as little as two weeks before they failed. Markets are prone to excessive exuberance in all dimensions—not just in the banking world. The question at issue is whether there is still something special about banks that deserves protection.

Today's banks—not all banks and not most banks, but some of the biggest banks—are different. If you want an extreme version of that, look at Bankers Trust. There is a bank with only a few deposits and with a few loans—maybe 15 percent of the balance sheet. Off-balance-sheet items are far larger than on-balance-sheet items, and I'm not sure they are completely understood by anybody in terms of what happens in really severe scenarios of pressure. The big banks are rapidly combining with investment banks, so we have all that kind of risk traditionally insulated from commercial banking. Tomorrow, I think we'll almost undoubtedly have insurance combined with banks. Traditional commercial banking, whether it is within an institution like Morgan or Bankers Trust where it has declined internally, has declined precipitously as a percentage of all financial assets in the country.

What does that mean? Individual "banking" institutions are bigger and bigger, more and more international, more and more inextricably combined with what we used to think of as different industries. Where does that lead us in this balance of market discipline, government support? What kind of supervision is appropriate? How far does the supervision go?

I regret John Heimann isn't here, who was also on the panel, because he is representative of one of these institutions that is not called a bank, but looks a lot like these other big institutions we still call banks. But, we do have three wise men, and I turn, first of all, to Carter Golembe.

Carter H. Golembe[*]

After almost 50 years of reasonable stability in banking, the distinguishing feature of the 1980s was, as George Hanc put it in his excellent paper, "the extraordinary upsurge in bank failures." It was a difficult time for everyone: the banks, the regulators, and the public. The intention now is to learn from and apply the lessons derived from studying the 1980s in order to avoid having to face banking problems of similar magnitude in the future and, more broadly, to enable the banking agencies and the banks to deal more knowledgeably and confidently with future problems. Clearly, this is a worthwhile exercise, and all of those responsible for initiating and conducting it deserve congratulations. I have a cautionary observation, plus several suggestions for future work.

My observation is really a reminder; certainly it is not new. It is to remember that from the same set of data or facts, analysts may draw dramatically different conclusions. Often the reason for this is that the future problems to which the lessons will be applied may be seen quite differently. The past can be intensely interesting, particularly for those who have lived through it, so much so that there is a danger of forgetting the most important point of all, which is that the problems of the past may have little or no resemblance to the problems of the future.

My hobby is reading military history, and I think I can say with some confidence that no profession spends more time than the military carefully going over past wars to identify mistakes and to prepare itself for the future, separating the strategies of enduring value from those soon to be irrelevant. This does not always work out well. No one spent more time than the French in their study of the bitter and immensely costly fighting during the four years of the first World War, from 1914 through 1918. The French applied the lessons of that war, as they perceived them, built the largest and best equipped army in the world, and then put it behind impregnable barriers. When war came again 20 years later and France was attacked, on May 10, 1940, it was completely defeated and capitulated in about six weeks. What happened?

First, in some important areas the French drew quite different conclusions from those drawn by the Germans, who had studied the same set of facts. The French became so obsessed with the past they forgot that the next war might be

* Carter H. Golembe is President of GHC Consulting, Inc., and before that was, respectively, Chairman of the Secura Group, and of Golembe Associates, Inc., both financial services consulting firms. From 1951 to 1960, he was a financial economist with the FDIC.

quite different. There is little question that if the war of 1914-18 had been resumed in 1939-40, the French would have been easy victors. Their fatal mistake was to forget that it might be a much different war—and it was.

I wish I could say with some confidence what future banking problems might be. I cannot. Of course there will be similarities with those that have been faced in the 1980s but there will also be differences. In fact, these differences might be so great as to render useless, or at best questionable, at least a few of the lessons likely to be drawn from a study of the 1980s, while at the same time pinpointing others of special value. The key question is: which?

I was delighted to find that the panel's assignment is to discuss "The 1980s in Retrospect." My dictionary defines "in retrospect" to mean "upon reflection," or "looking back on past events," which I hope gives me the liberty to go back a bit in history in the course of my reflections. I found the paper by George Hanc to be particularly useful in this regard: a readable summary of the findings of the study conducted by the FDIC. His paper covers the economic, legislative, and regulatory background of the bank failure experience of the 1980s, along with the regulatory and supervisory issues raised by that experience. Reflecting on it, I decided that those who had put this program together must have proceeded on a basic assumption: deposit insurance will continue more or less in its present form. But this is hardly likely to be the case; deposit insurance has changed continually over the past 60 years and will continue to do so. The fact that a primary, probably principal, reason for its creation was to help preserve a fragmented banking structure virtually guarantees this, since we are now in the midst of rapid consolidation of that structure. Moreover, deposit insurance, particularly the way it operates, is central to much of what is discussed in the FDIC's studies; key pieces of FDICIA, for example, reflect an explicit effort to protect the deposit insurance funds.

George's paper contains a statement that perhaps illustrates better why I think the study's underlying assumption is important. Discussing the collapse of the S&L insurance system, George points out that the hands of the authorities were tied by the shrinkage of their deposit insurance fund, noting that "one obvious conclusion" to be derived from this is that "an adequate insurance fund is a prerequisite for any attempt to control moral hazard." He is correct of course, but there are many other possible conclusions, such as that a different type of deposit insurance, not dependent on or tied to a deposit insurance fund, might be called for. Indeed, some of the most successful depositor protection systems we ever had in the United States—Indiana and Ohio before the Civil War for 30–40 years—were not based on an insurance fund.

The basic assumption that I think underlies the study can be broken into at least three parts. First, it is assumed that deposits in banks and in other institutions accepting deposits or near-deposits will continue to be protected by the federal government up to a specified amount, probably at least as large ($100,000 per depositor) as now. This I think is a reasonable assumption, even though there is no reason to believe that the same kind of protection could not be provided without the involvement of the government. In fact, there is a growing body of evidence to support this. Politically, however, this would be a difficult change to make and thus, as a betting man, I would say it is 10 to 1 or better that government will still be the guarantor 10 years from now.

The second part of the assumption is that the way in which the insurance or government guarantee is implemented will continue to be about the same as that followed today. This is much more questionable; I doubt that depositors care much, if at all, how they receive their protection, so long as it is received, and will not raise objections. The recent placing of more stringent limits on the ability of the FDIC to protect all depositors or all bank creditors is probably only the tip of the iceberg.

In 1935 the Corporation obtained legislation to inaugurate a quite reasonable program of encouraging those banks which had survived the debacle of 1932-33 but were still weak—banks had been permitted to join the new deposit insurance system with a minimum capital of $1—to merge with sounder banks. This program was reasonably successful for several years before being interrupted by World War II. After the war, it was discovered that the program was easily adaptable to handling, in addition to weak but solvent banks, those about to fail, enabling the FDIC to claim for a number of years that it had virtually eliminated bank failures (which were then defined as receiverships). In the mid-1950s, quite by accident, the FDIC discovered that it could also facilitate mergers after a bank was placed in receivership and, by the 1960s, the program began to be referred to as "purchase and assumption transactions." Such transactions were generally adopted by the FDIC for as many distressed banks as possible, in part because they provided 100 percent insurance protection.

In 1950 another important piece of legislation was obtained by the FDIC. Economists and others had predicted almost unanimously that the U.S. would face a great post-war depression after the end of World War II. The FDIC thought that this might lead to the failure of a number of large banks, which the deposit insurance fund would not be large enough to handle. Moreover, FDIC officials recalled that in the 1932-33 crisis the Federal Reserve had failed to assist a great many banks which, lacking such assistance, then failed. So the Corporation sought and obtained legislation enabling it to make loans to distressed banks without their having been merged out of existence or placed in receivership. The Federal Reserve was incensed at this request by the FDIC, regarding it as a transgression on its role as the nation's central bank and, in particular, as the "lender of last resort." Because of this opposition, as well as because the great post-war depression never happened, the FDIC did not make any use of this authority for about 20 years.

However, the Corporation crossed its own Rubicon in 1972 with a loan to the first billion-dollar bank to face failure (the Bank of the Commonwealth in Detroit), offering as justification, among other reasons, "the effect its closing might have had on public confidence in the nation's banking system." This was the beginning of the present "too-big-to-fail" program, although the FDIC had in fact long been following a policy of attempting to treat every bank in difficulty, regardless of size, as "too-big-to-fail." In any event, the program has assumed such dimensions that the President of the United States, no less, is now required by law to be consulted when disbursements for the purpose of saving a large bank are made.

It is useful to keep in mind that when it was created in 1933, the FDIC was asked to serve primarily as the paying agent for the government's deposit guarantee. All of the sophisticated paraphernalia that now exist—involving alternative methods of payment, open-bank assistance, closed-bank assistance, mergers, the treatment of very large banks etc.—came later. For the most part they came not because of a deliberate plan or adherence to specific banking policies, but incidentally or accidentally. Query: have they added very much value except to the size of the work force or the cost to the banking industry and to the government? If "yes," how relevant are they to the insurance function, as opposed, for example, to the lender-of-last-resort function? Or to the responsibilities of the chartering agencies?

The third element of the underlying assumption is that deposit insurance will continue to be provided in the future by an agency that also has authority to examine, supervise, and regulate banks. This is also questionable; I think the odds of it being the case ten years from now are probably about no better than even money. Once again, there are no political implications because depositor protection would not be altered; who does the actual regulating is not a matter that depositors know or care anything about.

Very shortly after the FDIC began operations, it asked for, and received, power to examine banks. Subsequently this authority was broadened and expanded, reaching its zenith, I hope, with FDICIA. But even from the outset, giving to an insuring agency the power to examine and regulate the banks whose deposits were insured was recognized as raising serious conflict-of-interest questions. In fact, the issue surfaced early in the Roosevelt administration.

Possibly there are some here who were in the audience in 1962 when the new FDIC building was dedicated and heard Wright Patman criticize the examination role of the FDIC, to the consternation of the officials on the dais. And in 1972-73, the separation of deposit insurance from bank supervision and regulation came within a hair of becoming fact; the Hunt Commission, solely because of its concern over the FDIC's conflict of interest, had recommended that the bulk of its supervision and regulatory responsibilities be transferred to another agency (to a new federal agency which, along with state agencies, would supervise and regulate state banks). With the overwhelming re-election of Mr. Nixon and the dedication of the Treasury Department to reform (in fact, it had created the Hunt Commission) it seemed quite likely that the recommendations would be adopted. But they were swept away by the tidal wave of Watergate.

Obviously this issue is still live. I was interested, but hardly surprised, to read in the paper on off-site surveillance systems that the "primary goal of bank supervision is to prevent losses to the deposit insurance fund." I believe that this is quite different from the way the objective would be described by many others engaged in the business of supervising banks.

The insurance agency, to be truly effective, probably must be something more than a mere paying agent. It would have to retain some minimum but essential regulatory functions, when Congress finally gets around to solving the conflict-of-interest problem. During the course of the debate over the administration's proposal several years ago to consolidate the FDIC, along with others, into a single new agency, thereby loosening the connection between insurance and examination, it is clear that the FDIC was giving its proposed new role some careful thought; I seem to recall a speech or possibly testimony by Director Hove on this subject. However, I did not sense in what I heard today, or read in the various study papers, that the consequences, for good or for ill, of separating the insurance function from the bank supervision function are being studied, and yet this separation could be part of the new world facing the FDIC.

William M. Isaac[*]

I think I'll go right into the subject Carter ended on. I think that Carter, you were using supervision and regulation sort of interchangeably, and I don't believe those are the same thing. A regulator approves corporate applications and powers and activities and the like. A supervisor conducts exams and/or looks over the shoulder of folks doing exams, takes enforcement actions, and the like. It was my view, while I was Chairman and since then, that the FDIC really ought to be a supervisor of banks and not a regulator of banks. I don't think it should be in the regulatory business. I was willing to give up the FDIC's regulatory powers when the Bush Task Force was deliberating these issues. I don't believe it matters to the FDIC whether a bank opens a new branch or not, and I don't think it matters to the FDIC whether a bank is in compliance with CRA and other such things. I don't believe that the FDIC ought to be dealing with anti-trust issues on mergers and the like. I believe firmly that this agency needs to be focused on the forest, not the trees. If we missed some things in the 1980s, I suspect it's because we were not stepping back and looking at the system and saying where is it going, what is happening, what is changing? The S&L industry is going like crazy—how is that going to impact banks?

I believe that is the kind of view and perspective the FDIC needs to be able to take and I think to do that it needs to be in all banks irrespective of their charter, whenever it chooses to be there. Hopefully not in an intrusive way, hopefully in coordination with the primary regulator. But I don't believe this agency ought to be restricted in any way from going wherever it needs to in the system to make sure it understands what is going on in that system and that the other agencies are doing their job. To me, it was unacceptable that the eighth largest bank in the country—Continental—was going down, and the FDIC had never been in the door before. I didn't think it was appropriate then and I don't think it is appropriate now, and don't think it will be appropriate in the future. This insurance agency, in my opinion, needs to be able to go where it needs to go, anytime it needs to go there, hopefully in coordination with the other agencies. It shouldn't matter what the charter is—it should only matter how big the bank is and what kinds of trends are evident in it.

---

* William M. Isaac is Chairman and Chief Executive Officer of The Secura Group, a financial institutions consulting firm. He served as Chairman of the FDIC from 1981 to 1985.

I wasn't going to spend my time, and I just wasted about two minutes of it, on that, but I really thought it was good to supplement what Carter said. I was hoping to focus a little bit on what I think is one of the FDIC's finest accomplishments during the 1980s, maybe in its history, and that is the way it handled the mutual savings bank problems. I first focused on the savings banks when I was still a director of the FDIC. I headed up a task force that was established to look at the savings bank problems. Some of the people in this room were involved in that task force. Because of the very, very high interest rates that were prevalent in the country, we saw a problem coming at us and we decided that we would prepare to deal with it. We did projections of the worst case, best case, most likely case scenario for interest rates; what that would mean for the FDIC's income; what that would mean in terms of savings bank failures in each of those cases; which banks would fail; how many months they had to live under the various scenarios. We had it all charted out, and I've got to tell you, if you look at that study today, it stands the test of time. It did forecast exactly what was going to happen under each of the scenarios.

We looked at the FDIC's investment policy and we decided it was too long on the maturities. The FDIC's maximum exposure to savings bank losses was going to be highest in a high-rate environment, so we needed to shorten maturities to maximize our income and liquidity in a high-rate environment. It was going to cost us money if rates declined, but that was all right because then our savings bank losses would be lower.

We had a big debate in the task force about how aggressive we should be in dealing with savings bank problems. The prevailing view, inside and outside of government at the time, was that this was a liquidity problem—I mean an interest-rate spread problem and not a solvency issue. All we needed to do was give these institutions a chance to get through this period of very high interest rates. We had to make sure they had the liquidity to get through this period, and if they did, they would be able to make it.

The FDIC task force had a different view. Our view was that the main thing we needed to do was to keep terminally ill savings banks from infecting healthier institutions. We didn't want to close down institutions needlessly. Bob Litan spoke earlier about the social cost of not taking prompt corrective action, and is there a social cost. But if we had marked-to-market accounting back in that period, and if we had wanted to, we could have closed every savings bank in the country at a cost to the FDIC of tens of billions of dollars. That is what the numbers were. We had it documented in the savings bank task force. So, we could have shut them all down, marked-to-market, and spent tens of billions of dollars. I say the social cost of that would have been inordinately high.

Instead, we decided to pursue what I considered a more reasonable course. We made a decision that we would adopt certain policies with respect to these savings banks to try to help them get through this period without infecting other institutions. So, what we said is our minimum capital standard is 5 percent tangible capital—that is our minimal standard. Any savings bank that drops below that floor will be monitored very, very closely and it will be put under operating restrictions. It will not be allowed to grow. It will not be allowed to pay up for deposits. It will not be able to enter into new activities. It will not be able to expand or in any way increase the risk exposure, the risk profile, of the institution. We instructed the savings banks to that effect. We told them that if they violated our rules, we would remove the management and if that didn't work, we would close the institution.

We also agreed that when an institution hit a book capital ratio of zero, we would close it. We would do a deal with a stronger institution with real FDIC financial assistance going in—no phony deals, no goodwill, just real money being spent to solve real problems. We would allow other institutions to bid, but those institutions had to be viable. The resulting entity after the deal was done had to be viable. We wouldn't put two or three weaklings together, hoping and praying that the merged firm would survive. That was our policy. It was pursued and what was a $150 billion industry with a potential insolvency of tens of billions of dollars was handled at a cost of roughly $1.8 billion.

The S&L policy was exactly the opposite. It was a policy of lower capital standards. It allowed massive amounts of goodwill, allowed weak institutions to merge, and allowed them to grow. If S&Ls could get bigger and add new assets bearing higher rates, the problems would go away—they'll bury the old assets with the new higher-yielding assets. It failed spectacularly. The S&L problem in 1980 or so was roughly the same type of problem and the same size problem relative to assets as we had in the savings bank industry. The savings bank problem was resolved for $1.8 billion; the S&L problem was resolved for $150 billion. They allowed the cancer to spread.

I believe that a series of governmental policies led to the failure of the S&L industry and cost the taxpayers $150 billion. Number one, the S&Ls were clearly in trouble in the 1970s. Banks should have been allowed to acquire them. They were not allowed to do so. Second, we ignored the Hunt Commission's recommendations for variable rates on the S&L loans, to phase out Regulation Q, and to allow thrifts to have broader asset powers. These recommendations were made in the early 1970s. If they had been implemented, we probably wouldn't have had a serious S&L problem in the 1980s.

Number two, we allowed inflation to get out of control during the 1970s due to rather aggressive or sloppy government monetary and fiscal policies, which led to the very high interest-rate period that necessarily had to follow. We had an abrupt withdrawal of Regulation Q once the rates went up, without having dealt with the asset deregulation first. There was no choice—it was either get rid of Reg. Q in a hurry or these institutions were going to fail anyway because they wouldn't have any liquidity.

Congress raised the deposit insurance limit to $100,000. The FDIC strongly objected to allowing the deposit insurance ceiling to go to $100,000 because weak institutions would be able to bid up for funds. There was no Reg. Q on those deposits. Weak institutions would be able to bid for the funds without any sort of discipline whatsoever from the market.

We had the abrupt change in tax policy with respect to real estate in 1986 to throw more fuel on the fire. These changes had a very negative effect on the viability of real estate projects already on the books of financial institutions.

I've already talked about how the government decided that the S&L problem was a liquidity problem—all we had to do was let them grow real fast and they would grow their way out of the problem. They would bury the old yielding assets with much higher yielding new assets. We had little or no regulation or supervision of marginal institutions. Institutions without capital were encouraged to grow. Finally, we had this terrible failure to deal with the issue of brokered deposits. Money brokers were going around the country sweeping up hundreds of billions of dollars of funds, dumping them into the institutions that paid the highest rates. Most of those were S&Ls. My guess is this raised the cost of the S&L crisis by some $50 billion. The FDIC and the FSLIC tried to stop that abuse of the system by eliminating pass-through deposit insurance coverage. We were sued by the money brokers and they won in court. They said we didn't have authority to adopt the regulation. We asked Congress for relief, and all Congress did was criticize us for picking on the poor Wall Street firms. The Wall Street firms were charging fees to gather up that money. They were charging the institutions that bought the money a fee. Then they were taking the money that those institutions collected and investing it in junk bonds to fund the LBO deals that the investment banking firms were putting together. There were some investment bankers that earned as much as $500 million a year—and I'm talking about individuals—and it was clearly made possible through a massive abuse of the deposit insurance system. I think the problems in the S&L industry were foreseeable. They were foreseen. I think the problems in the S&L industry affected much of the banking system. I suspect we wouldn't have had nearly the problems in the banking system had we not had an S&L crisis.

I'm at my ten minutes and I will need to stop at this point.

John G. Medlin, Jr.[*]

I'm delighted to be here with this distinguished panel of friends and observers of banking—the younger one of the group, I think, of these old timers from the 80s. There is not a lot I add at this point to all that has been said today and all that is in the papers except a blinding flash or two of the obvious. The bottom line is that the fortunes of banks and their performance are determined largely by three basic factors. One is public policy. The second is the condition and performance of the economy. The third is management practices, internal management of those institutions.

We've talked a lot about public policies and to boil the problem down in a one-liner—what we had, and to some extent what we still have, is the democratization of credit—the democratization and liberalization of credit to everyone, cheaper credit, more liberal credit, but in the final analysis, the socialization of the risks underlying that credit falls ultimately back on the people. We have some other things like that—we have Medicare and we have Social Security which are actuarially unsound and ultimately will cause problems and deposit insurance is not a problem as long as times are good. It is only when we have unusual times like the 80s that it becomes a problem.

Also, public policies were relaxed and changed in all ill-timed way, as several have described. Raising deposit insurance to $100,000 just before removing interest-rate limitations was a huge mistake. A lot of bankers look back on their figures for the 1980s and say, gosh, we did a terrific job. Well, the reason they did a terrific job is because it was a no-brainer time for growing deposits. You put a sign up on a busy corner that said "Insured by FDIC" and people would stop by and leave money. They even mailed it in, or if you didn't want to go to that much trouble, you could broker it in, as Bill said—$100,000 pieces from the Indian tribes and whoever else had a computer program to send money from all over the country.

Economic history will record the 1980s deposit growth in banks and thrifts as an anomaly. We have never in history had those kinds of savings flow into banking. Historically, bank deposits have come largely from three sources: transaction money; parked money that somebody is going to need—and they park it in the

* John G. Medlin, Jr. is Chairman of the Board of Directors of Wachovia Corporation. He was Chief Executive Officer of Wachovia Corporation from 1976 through 1993.

bank for a while; and from small savers who don't have enough for more sophisticated investments.

Traditionally, those with larger amounts of longer-term savings have invested more in other media like stocks and bonds or mutual funds. That was not true in the 80s. We had this huge flow of money into banks and thrifts first because Congress said it was guaranteed by the federal government. One way or the other people believed the full faith and credit declaration for the thrift fund also applied to the FDIC fund. Secondly, during most of that decade, we had a negative or relatively flat yield curve, which meant that money market accounts or CDs of banks and thrifts often had a yield as good or better than long governments.

So, large investors as well as small savers were smart—they said, my gosh, I don't need to go into those other market instruments, like stocks and bonds and risk market value loss. I'll just put it in the bank and do better than elsewhere. That was true until we got to the late 80s and early 90s when the yield curve became positive and money started trickling out of banks and thrifts in search of higher returns. The money that was bailed out by the FSLIC and the FDIC, where is it now? Much of it is in mutual funds—those permanent savings that trickled out. Since the late 80s bank consumer deposit growth has been anemic. If you take off the interest credit, they have actually shrunk. Mutual fund balances now exceed total consumer deposits in banks, thrifts, and credit unions.

As Carter said, I think in some respects we may be preparing for the wrong war. The problem that regulated and insured financial institutions face looking ahead is a funding problem. Part of the problem back in the 80s was that they had the tremendous inflow of money burning a hole in their pocket and they went out and lent it—unfortunately, not very wisely.

Management practices—banking can't blame public policy, can't blame the economy really for its problems. It can blame itself for failing to exercise proper private sector disciplines. We should have learned to expect public policies not to be very smart—in most times—very politically driven, very expediently driven. In the management side of this equation, we had competition in laxity. Unfortunately the dumbest and weakest competitors in the marketplace set the basic standards of pricing and credit terms. We developed what I call a stretch sock pricing approach that said one rate fits all—no risk discrimination. This is where the real problem comes.

An old timer in the credit program at Wachovia that I went through in 1959 said there are no loans we won't make that aren't illegal, immoral or unethical, but there are lots of people who won't pay the price that the risk demands. It is true—there aren't any bad loans when they are made but interest rates sometimes are too low to cover the risk. They just go bad and if you are able to put enough away in reserves, you could charge off loans where you have a 40 percent interest rate and 30 percent charge-offs and come out very well. Today, you can look back at the 80s and say the problem was pricing, not the loans that were made. Proper pricing means that some real estate projects won't be economic if the loans to finance them are priced at the rate that properly reflects the risk. That is where banking went wrong in the 80s.

Also, and it is probably more popular now than back in the 80s, problems can arise from syndication or selling out pieces of loans, where the syndicator takes a nice fee for putting it together, but sells it off and keeps very little risk. A syndication is sometimes characterized as a transfer of risk from someone who lacks courage to someone who lacks knowledge. There is an enormous amount of that going on today—most smaller banks do not have the capability to assess the syndicated risks they are putting on their books.

I think our greatest lesson from the 80s would be complacency, and probably our greatest risk today is complacency. Everything is wonderful; the economy is wonderful; public policies have gotten better in many respects, but have managements learned their lessons? You look at the balance sheet of banking, as reported by the FDIC for September 30, and you see on the surface adequate capital of $370 billion, loss reserves of about $50 billion, so $420 billion of capital and reserves to cushion about $2.5 trillion of loans. But, you look further and you see approximately $2.5 trillion of unused loan commitments. Remember I said there may be a funding problem. You can also see $20 trillion of derivatives exposure, off balance sheet. If other off-balance-sheet exposures were reported, you would see foreign currencies and a bunch of other things that aren't reflected. There is not $20 trillion of risk in those derivatives, but, say, there is only 5 percent or 6 percent or 7 percent, which is probably more accurate. It is still $1 trillion or more of risk and you begin to not be so impressed with that capital ratio.

The economy gets leveraged today more in off-balance-sheet-type risks than in actual loans-outstanding risk, and this is the war I think regulators should be preparing for—being able to analyze and understand and help management see all the other risks that are being taken that aren't explicit on the balance sheet.

Another thing that old timer in my credit school said, you can't extinguish risk—you can only transfer it to another party. Actually, all derivatives and other such things do is diffuse risk and spread it out across the system, but does that risk accumulate on the backs of the weaker or the stronger participants in the marketplace? Who knows—we will find out. But the ability for all this risk to be permanently transferred depends on the ability of the transferee to absorb it in adverse times. Otherwise, in most cases, it comes trotting back like a hungry little puppy dog at the time when the crisis hits, as Paul Volcker well knows from some of his big ones that he wrestled over. So, I would say my time is up—a little over. But, let's not be complacent and let's not let ourselves be blinded by some of the better aspects of the financial landscape at this point.

Volcker: We have 25 minutes, by our imposed deadline, for discussion, and I want to invite people out there to discuss. To expedite things, let me ask a few questions of these experts which may be on your minds and that have come up earlier. Is there any role for private insurance? I don't think it was getting very good notices earlier in the day. But, in a marginal sense, if you had FDIC insurance for 90 percent of the deposits, is there any room for somebody else taking the other 10 percent or something like that?

Subordinated debt did arise and was a favorite proposal of yours, Bill. I thought it made a lot of sense ten years ago. Do you still think it makes a lot of sense in the context that Bob Litan was raising earlier?

Marked-to-market accounting, Bill had a rather sour comment about that; Bob had a rather favorable comment about it. Is your comment really sour? Does it really make any sense?

Just to express my own biases, I think, pushed to an extreme, it is nonsense for a bank. The idea that we have to be so precise about marked-to-market accounting for an institution that is supposed to take liquid funds and transform it into something longer, while we tolerate enormous uncertainties in accounting on other parts of the balance sheet and in industry generally, doesn't make sense to me. An accounting profession that will tolerate company after company taking large accounting losses for prospective events or to account for past losses that didn't appear on the balance sheet the day before, and doesn't blink an eyelash, shouldn't worry too much about marked-to-market accounting, in my opinion. Those were the three questions I had.

Golembe: I'll take the insurance one. What I said about insurance was that first of all, I think there is a role for private insurance. I am not at all convinced that you could not have as good, if not a better, insurance system, run privately. But, what I was talking about, Paul, is politically I think it is impossible. Since it is impossible politically, I just didn't want to waste much time on it.

One other point I made that I might elaborate on—not all deposit insurance systems in this country have relied on an insurance fund. The two most successful, in Indiana and Ohio—30 or 40 years in each case—before the Civil War were the most successful insurance we ever had. They did not rely on a deposit insurance fund. They relied on cross guarantee by the banks—Indiana, for example, did not have a bank failure in 35 years. The head of the Indiana insurance system became the first Comptroller of the Currency. We've never had since as successful a system as we had then in those two states.

Volcker: I suspect nobody in this room will challenge you on your historical analysis of Indiana before the Civil War.

Isaac: Subordinated debt—in 1982 we did a study called Deposit Insurance in a Changing Environment. We were concerned that interest rates were being deregulated and deposit insurance was not being dealt with. We were increasing the moral hazard by deregulating interest rates without modifying the deposit insurance system to bring some greater degree of deposit or discipline. We suggested, in a very nice book that Congress ignored, how you might change the deposit insurance system to deal with this growing moral hazard. One of the ideas that we thought made a lot of sense was the subordinated debt idea. We wouldn't necessarily increase capital requirements, but we would mandate that some portion of it be in subordinated debt so that you would have sophisticated creditors overseeing banks and deciding who could get subordinated debt at what price and who couldn't. I thought it made a lot of sense at the time. The reason why we thought it was an interesting idea was because we thought that other changes to the deposit insurance system were not in the political cards. It was unlikely that Congress, having increased the deposit insurance limit to $100,000 two years earlier, would reduce the deposit insurance limit below $100,000 again. So, why not go ahead and concede defeat on depositor discipline and try to impose it through sophisticated creditor discipline. I think it made sense at the time, and I think it still could make sense today. It is an admission of defeat that you can't change the deposit insurance system. It would be, in my opinion, far more desirable if we could find the political will to change the deposit insurance system by imposing discipline on depositors over $100,000. I believe you can do that without cratering the world. I also think you can probably make the $100,000 limit less of a problem by, for example, allowing a $100,000 limit per social security number. Right now a family can take the $100,000 limit and turn it into over a million dollar limit quite easily.

So, I think that the idea of subordinated debt makes sense. I would rather deal with deposit insurance limits and the way the system operates, but if we can't, then I think subordinated debt is an idea that we need to consider.

I think marked-to-market accounting is a very bad idea whose time should never come.

Medlin: I think it would be possible to design an insurance system that could work if you could get the laws passed that would enable you to enforce the conditions that would make it work, and that is probably not possible. Market value accounting—it has its virtues, but at the same time, it is a problem in times of stress when you have to market at the worst possible condition when if you could disguise it for awhile, things would be okay. As we have learned from our own banking system, if the thrifts who stuck in there and didn't sell their low rate mortgages when rates were high survived and the ones that bailed out went broke. So, subordinated debt is something that has its place as long as you recognize what it is and what it isn't.

Isaac: I just want to say one thing about marked-to-market. First of all, I think if you had marked the savings banks to market, clearly the FDIC would have been out tens of billions of dollars. But also let's take the LDC debt crisis, which was mentioned earlier. As you know, it was a massive problem. There was no market for LDC debt, so if you had tried to mark those loans to market, you would have driven almost every money-center bank into insolvency at the same time. I have trouble understanding how that would have been good for America.

Volcker: In a situation in which it wasn't at all clear that most of those loans could not be eventually be repaid, as they in fact were, marking to market in the middle of the crisis would have driven down the price even further, as subsequently happened.

Isaac: Right, so the question is—do you mark the balance sheet and the income sheet to market, or do you understand what the market values are and deal appropriately with those institutions that have a problem, like we did with the savings banks.

Volcker: Let me make your point in the way I would have made it, because I think it is the same thing. You've got items on both sides of the balance sheet that have readily ascertainable market values. It is a trading institution, a typical dealer, sure you want a marked-to-market. Dealers typically operate on very thin capital requirements and are permitted to do so by the market as well as by regulators, appropriately so. If everything is liquid, then mark-to-market.

A bank, by design, at least in the old days, was not supposed to be highly liquid in that same sense—100 percent of the balance sheet or even close to it on both sides liquid. It was supposed to take relatively liquid deposits and transform them into something longer. An extreme and an unreasonable case, in terms of prudent banking, was the LDC debt crisis. That was taking what banks are supposed to be doing to an extreme and until the crisis it would not have been reflected in marked-to-market accounting. That is why, in concept, the institution is supervised—so that you can make some appraisal of what they're doing. I think in those circumstances, you don't drive a doctrinaire view of marked-to-market accounting to the wall. I think we probably go too far in other financial institutions in that respect.

Be that as it may, what questions do you have out there.

Question: What is unique about North Carolina's banking laws or the atmosphere that produced three large regional banks when you don't see that sort of production in any other state in the union?

Medlin: The first thing is that we have had statewide branch banking since the Civil War—since the banking system got reestablished after the Civil War. There were communities that were poor and wanted banks, so banks were encouraged to expand across the state rather than being kept out. That is the first thing. So, we had statewide banking. We developed into a very healthy system of several banks which are statewide. Some are regional within the east or the west or the middle part of the state, and most communities of any size have one or two hometown community banks that don't have branches anywhere else. The larger banks are progressive and responsible and there is healthy competition. There is an occasional reckless renegade who ends up looking silly and paying for it. So, North Carolina is just a good, sound banking state. I don't know that our banking laws have been very different except for the branching laws.

Question: I'm Bob Miailovich. I would like to ask a question that really has to do specifically with capital, but it falls within the area of regulation versus supervision that Bill Isaac brought up. I think one of the major legacies of the time period we are talking about is the fact that for the first time in our history, we legislated capital requirements, that until the International Lending Supervision Act required and set a specific number, it was strictly supervisory, more of a discussion between examiners and bankers and so forth. We now have this very elaborate system of risk-based capital, and I read recently some voices at the Federal Reserve are already admitting that it is not covering everything and we need to go back and look at some finer tuning and maybe rely back on the bank's own justification for their capital levels for part of this business. Are we stuck with this, in your opinion? We have heard some good defenses today for PCA. First of all, I think most people who have been talking about it have been talking about the 2 percent closing. They have not been talking about the early intervention before then. But, it strikes me that is a major legacy that we are left with—are these laws and regulations trying to set capital numbers, and then the regulator is trying to know how to measure it. I would be interested in your comments about what do we do with that legacy and if we come back in 20 years, are we still going to have laws that mandate numbers?

Volcker: I was glad to hear you raise that question because it struck me there is relatively little talk here about capital and there has been, I think, a dramatic change between the beginning of the 80s and the second half of the 80s in capital requirements. Have we deliberately or otherwise stumbled upon a tool of banking regulation and supervision that indeed can go a long way toward preventing a recurrence of what happened in the 80s? Before the new requirements, there had been a long period of erosion of capital in the very informal way it was dealt with by the regulators at that time. Who wants to comment on that? It also has international dimensions, I might say. This is the first time we have this kind of international consistency.

Isaac: Actually, I think that one of the better things that has come out is that we have imposed capital standards of some sort throughout the world and I think part of the pressure on U.S. banks, particularly the major ones, was that they were facing competitors from around the world that had no capital, and therefore didn't much care about pricing, particularly those that were sponsored by their government. So, I think that imposing some capital minimums around the world wasn't a bad idea. I hate to see it in statutory form because you never know when you're going to need to get rid of it. I think prompt, corrective action is a huge mistake. Not the concept of prompt corrective action. Certainly regulators ought to be prompt in correcting problems they see and slowing institutions down. But I think doing everything by the numbers without discretion is a mistake. People keep on pushing for marked-to-market accounting, prompt corrective action and the like, and the next time we have an ag-bank crisis or a savings bank crisis or an LDC debt crisis, I think we are going to regret we have those laws on the books. I think it is going to tie the regulators' hands in a way that is going to precipitate a crisis, that could otherwise be avoided.

Volcker: You are objecting to the rigidity of it?

Isaac: The concept of prompt corrective action has been one of the hallmarks of the FDIC for a long time. So, the FDIC likes lots of capital, but the rigidity of the system I believe we are going to come to regret. But we're probably not politically astute enough or brave enough to get rid of it until it causes us a big problem.

Golembe: In answer to Bob's question that yes, we're stuck with it. Probably the greatest risk we face at the next crisis, whenever it will be, is that FDICIA will not have been repealed.

Question: As you well know, more and more loan categories are being structured for sale. As I understand it, commercial real estate loans are now marked-to-market. Do you believe that loans for which there is a market should be marked-to-market? I can understand why loans that you have to send teams of accountants in to evaluate what they might be worth under some set of circumstances shouldn't be marked-to-market, but what about loans that are traded?

Volcker: I am speaking for myself and I'm not going to get into enormous detail, but in general I would feel if you can value an asset reasonably, and even if you can't, it is incumbent to make some kind of an estimate of what that value might be in your annual or other report, which has been a practice for a long time. That is not quite the same as saying, I know the value so well, I'm going to actually adjust the balance sheet. But, if it is an important discrepancy, you ought to footnote it. At some point, maybe you ought to mark it to market if you are about to sell it or you have it for sale, which is a distinction the current rules make.

Isaac: You've got a lot of the balance sheet that can't be marked to market in any sort of a sensible way, and what are you going to do about the liability side. How are you going to mark it to market? It is really tough.

Volcker: It is really complicated.

Isaac: There are also a lot of assets in the bank that are not on the balance sheet at all. For example, Citicorp—what is their credit card operation worth that is not reflected on that balance sheet? So, if people want to mark things to market, you're going into a morass. I've got to tell you, when we were dealing with the savings bank problem, I was thinking seriously about how you could mark their balance sheets to market, so I was actually at one point sort of a proponent. I finally decided that it was a bad idea whose time should never come.

Question: Following up on the last discussion on rules versus discretion, if the Congress were to offer you a deal along the following lines—we will repeal all of the rules regarding capital and prompt corrective action, and restore supervisory and regulatory discretion, in return for a single consolidated regulatory agency outside the Treasury, outside the Fed, and outside the FDIC, is that a deal worth making?

Volcker: Everybody here has either been in the Treasury or the Federal Reserve or the FDIC, so they don't want to make the deal. You want a new agency outside all the present three?

Isaac: I have no qualms about the present system, except that I do think the FDIC ought to be focused on its insurance and liquidation responsibilities and not try to be a regulator. I must say, I believe the bank regulators—and I'm not saying that just because I'm in a room full of bank regulators—I believe the bank regulators did one terrific job in containing a massive set of problems in the 1980s. You weren't going to prevent a bunch of farm banks from going broke when we had an agricultural depression. There were going to be some farm banks going broke. When you have a massive collapse of the real estate industry like we had on the heels of the S&L crisis and the tax law changes and everything else, you're going to have some bank failures. You can't prevent that. All you can do is try to contain them and spot some of the trends before they get too far out. I also think it is a regulator's job to lean against whatever wind is blowing at the time. If everybody is doing really well and they are putting on a bunch of loans in real estate, that is the time to be saying, I wonder why they are putting on all those loans in real estate—maybe we ought to be taking a much closer look at it. That is very tough to do—to go into a major bank before it has obvious problems and say, you guys are making a lot of real estate loans and we are really worried about it and we think you ought to slow down. I've seen it. I was in Security Pacific on behalf of that board of directors, looking at what happened and why. The Comptroller of the Currency actually was calling the thing at Security Pacific five or six years before it happened, before it blew up. They kept on saying, you're doing this, you're doing that, and Security Pacific would write back and say—we appreciate your kind note, but frankly, we are Security Pacific—you don't seem to understand that—and please keep in touch. That was the end of that. What are you going to do about it?

Volcker: I don't like the way you posed the question—as a trade for discretion. Whatever you think about independent banking agencies, I wouldn't tie the issue to discretion. I always thought the strength of the Federal Reserve as a regulator and a supervisor—not everybody may think it had strength, but I thought it was fairly well borne out in the 1980s—rests on the fact it can better resist the industry pressure, precisely because regulation and supervision are not its sole responsibility. I think a single-purpose agency, combined with the discretion, makes it even more vulnerable to the kind of pressure that Bill was talking about, that will be true on capital requirements or anything else. It is just harder when so much of your existence, in some sense, depends upon your relationships with the regulated.

Golembe: I always preferred the Hunt Commission approach, which was not a single agency but two agencies, rather than three. So, you would still have the two, but then you would have the FDIC focus simply on insurance, which I think is what Bill was talking about. I thought that was a good recommendation.

Question: I want to ask one final question because in his recent piece in the *American Banker* Bill Isaac called for abolishing the too big to fail concept. So, I would like to zero in on Continental. If you had it to do all over again, do you believe it was a mistake for the FDIC to assist in keeping Continental open, and I would like the other panelists to comment on Bill's comments.

Isaac: Actually, I was just talking about that the other day with a banker who asked that very question. Before I get into this answer, let me thank you for putting on this wonderful conference. You really stimulated me, and I'm going to write a paper that I will submit to the conference officials. It occurred to me that I never put down on paper what happened in the 80s from my perspective, and I'm going to do that now. But, anyway, the way I feel about Continental is this—if you gave me the same set of facts today that I had then, and the same knowledge of what was going on and what was likely to go on, I would do the same thing all over again. I think we did effect a good solution. We maintained stability in the system. It was a very low-cost solution to a massive problem.

What I was looking at is that we had a bunch of small banks that would have failed, but what I was really concerned about—and I know Paul was—is that Manny Hanny goes down, B of A goes down, First Chicago goes down, all the Texas banks go down, the entire S&L industry collapses all at once. So you have all this massive hemorrhaging throughout the country's financial system—everything comes down at once and what do we do about it. That was what the fear was. I think it was a fear that was legitimate. I think there was a substantial chance that a lot of that would have occurred.

What I never counted on, though, was that all those things would happen anyway—or a lot of those things would happen anyway—and that the S&L problem would be allowed to grow from a $15 billion problem at that time to a $150 billion problem. I look back now and I say, wait a minute, what if we had allowed Continental to go down and all these bad things started happening—what could possibly have occurred that would have cost more than $150 billion to fix. I can't think of anything we could have done that would have cost more than $150 billion to fix.

Volcker: Let me give you a little perspective on this that I think is going to the heart of the whole discussion today. I agree with Bill's decision, obviously, and the Federal Reserve decision which were combined. That came at a particularly critical point. It was in the middle of the debt crisis and there was worry about other banks and the economy was in deep recession and so forth and so on. I think it was necessary. But, in fact, it had a big effect—that was the precursor of a lot of protection that happened afterwards. I can remember looking at television when I was out of office in 1990 and 1991 and 1992—and it would be in the press every day—that so-and-so bank or savings and loan was close to insolvent and failing, and nobody seemed to care. Even when you had headlines about the weakness of an institution no depositors moved their money because they had been convinced that the government was going to take care of everything, so you had no market discipline. It drives the lesson that has been described here over and over again. How do you get some balance between the rescue and retaining some discipline? I don't know whether we yet have the right answer.

Isaac: The other thing that I would make clear is that the way we handled Continental was determined way back in 1982 when Penn Square failed. We thought then that Continental might happen and we said to ourselves, if Penn Square causes some of these larger banks like SeaFirst and Continental to go down, we will stop it there. We are not going to stop it here at Penn Square— we are going to make some people pay the price for Penn Square. But, we will deal with the ripple effects on these much larger banks if and when they do occur. So when Paul called me and asked me to come over to talk about the $10 billion overnight run on Continental, we didn't have any debate—we knew exactly what we were going to do. There was no discussion of should we do it, wringing of hands or anything else—we knew we were going to stop it there.

Volcker: We have reached the magic hour. I had another comment I was going to make. You won't be able to resolve it for me but I'll raise it anyway. It strikes me that when one looks at the banking system, never before in our lifetime has the industry been under so much competitive pressure with declining market share in many areas and a feeling of intense strain, yet at the same time, the industry never has been so profitable with so much apparent strength. How do I reconcile those two observations?

It has been a pleasure to be here.